# The Yoruba People

*A Captivating Guide to the History of the Yorubas and Yoruba Mythology*

# Free Bonus from Captivating History
# (Available for a Limited time)

Hi History Lovers!

Now you have a chance to join our exclusive history list so you can get your first history ebook for free as well as discounts and a potential to get more history books for free! Simply visit the link below to join.

Captivatinghistory.com/ebook

Also, make sure to follow us on Facebook, Twitter and Youtube by searching for Captivating History.

# Contents

# Introduction

*The Yoruba People: A Captivating Guide to the History of the Yorubas and Yoruba Mythology* is not just a collection of events. It is a detailed compilation of the culture, history, practices, and legends that form the experiences of the Yoruba people. This book will serve as an excellent foundation to better understand how the ethos of the ancient Yorubas shaped the lives of the present Yoruba people.

According to a study carried out at the University of Florida, there are twenty-five million Yoruba people globally. Some scholars argue that there are over fifty million Yoruba people, with Nigeria alone having an estimated population of about forty million. The disparity in these figures may be due to the fact that many Yoruba people have migrated from West Africa and now live in almost every country all over the world. But who exactly are the Yoruba people? Where did they originate? What language do they speak, and where can they be found? You can expect to find the answers to all of these questions and more in this book.

Read how the lifestyle of the Yoruba people changed but still manages to contain elements of their forefathers. Let this book take you on a journey that spans over fifteen centuries!

*Let's get started.*

# Chapter 1 – Yoruba: The Origins

*A Brief Introduction to the Yoruba People*

To start with, the word Yoruba, pronounced "yaw-roo-buh," is used to describe both a language and an ethnic group. Therefore, it is difficult to speak about the Yoruba people without discussing the language itself. The Yoruba people can be primarily found in Nigeria, Benin, and Togo, as they originated from these countries. As mentioned earlier, due to their high rate of emigration, they can also be found in other places and have high residency rates in countries like Ghana, the United States, the United Kingdom, Italy, and Canada.

*Where the Yoruba people initially settled*

Interestingly, the term Yoruba was not always used for the Yoruba-speaking people. In fact, it didn't officially come into use until the 19ᵗʰ century. The Hausa people originally used the word Yoruba to reference the Oyo people of Nigeria. The Hausas, who are well known for their nomadic habits, popularized the name during their travels all over West Africa.

Prior to Yoruba being used as the standardized term to describe the entire ethnic group, they were known by different names in different regions. One of the many names ascribed to them is Aku, which was taken from the first word in their greetings—*E ku aaro*, meaning "good morning," and *E ku ale*, meaning "good night."

Another term used for the Yoruba people is Okun, which is a slight variation of *Aku*, and *Anago* or *Nago*, which was derived from the Yoruba group in the Republic of Benin. Lucumi, which was derived from *o luku mi*, meaning "my friend," was another term used to describe the Yorubas in Cuba and some other Spanish-speaking countries.

Prior to these terms, the Yorubas described themselves as *omo Oduduwa*, meaning "the children of Oduduwa," referencing the man who is believed to be the founding father of the Yorubas. They also describe themselves as *omo Karo-oojiire*, meaning "the people who ask good morning, did you wake up well?" The reason for this term is due to the well-practiced act of greeting others in the Yoruba culture. The Yorubas have a specific greeting for any situation. For example, *E ku ewa o* is used to salute hairstylists while they are performing a service, and *E ku ewu omo o* is used to praise mothers who have just given birth.

The Yoruba language is said to have developed out of the Volt-Niger branch of the Niger-Congo group of languages. It is classified among the Edekiri languages, which include the Yoruba languages, the Ede dialect, and Itsekiri. These languages are spoken across Togo, Nigeria, and Benin. Some believe that the Yoruba language has over forty million speakers in Nigeria. It is the most spoken African language outside of Africa.

For those interested in linguistics, the Yoruba language can be further divided into five dialects: Southeast, Northeast, Southwest, Northwest, and Central. There are many variations existing within these five major dialects, with a thin line differentiating them from one another. For instance, the Northwest Yoruba dialect includes sub-dialects such as Oyo, Lagos, Ibadan, Egba, and Yewa, while the Northeast dialect consists of the sub-dialects of Abunu, Yagba, and Ijumu. Interestingly, the Yoruba language spoken in these five major regions differs greatly, and it may be difficult for some of these people to understand each other.

# Accounts of Creation

The Yoruba culture is primarily oral, which means history was passed down through stories, legends, and folklore. In the Yoruba culture, the families responsible for telling the stories had to be appointed by the king, and the role of historian was inherited by the family member who received the most training or knew the most stories. As to be expected, the stories vary.

Just as the scientific world has a widely accepted theory of creation (the Big Bang), the Yorubas have their own account of creation. Although, it is probably more accurate to say accounts since there is more than one accepted version. The first and most widely popular account of creation is told as follows.

In the beginning, the whole universe was made up of the sky above and the water below. The entire surface of the earth was covered in water. Olodumare, the king of the heavens or the supreme being, sent down some divine beings to establish life on earth. While preparing for this journey, Olodumare gave them one chicken, a calabash (a type of gourd) containing sand, and one palm nut. These heavenly beings descended to earth by a chain and landed on the spot known as Ife, which is regarded as the heart of Yorubaland. The heavenly beings poured the sand on the surface of the water and placed the chicken on it. As the chicken began to scratch the sand with its claws, the sand began to spread until it formed the islands and continents of the world.

Another account of this story states that the heavenly beings went with a chameleon, and as the fowl spread the sand over the earth, the chameleon determined if the land was dry and solid enough. It is also believed that the areas still covered with water are those places not touched by the sand. The heavenly beings planted the palm nut, and it grew into the plants we have today. The human race was said to have descended from the heavenly beings where it all started, in Ile-Ife. This creation account implies that the Yorubas were the first humans and that other humans and civilizations originated from Nigeria.

Another notable creation story similar to the one above states that when Oduduwa, popularly known as the Father of Yorubaland, was sent to create humankind, he was given a chicken and a bag of sand. As he descended down a long chain, he lost his grip on the chicken. While attempting to catch the falling chicken, he lost his grip on the bag of sand. The sand plummeted, and by the time Oduduwa recovered, the sand had already formed a mound, with the chicken seated atop it. The sand started expanding, and he exclaimed, "Ile n'fe!" meaning "The land is expanding!"

Another slightly different creation account states that Olodumare sent a group of heavenly beings on an expedition. According to this account, Olodumare made Obatala the leader of this expedition, but along the way, Obatala got drunk and fell into a drunken stupor. Due to this, Oduduwa had to take over the expedition, and he subsequently completed the mission, thus making him the father of the Yoruba people and all the people of the world.

Another version says that the Yorubas migrated from Mecca and were descended from Lamurudu, one of the kings of Mecca. One of Lamurudu's offspring is Oduduwa, who is the ancestor of the Yoruba people. However, this version did not state the period when

Lamurudu was in power, but it talks about the revolution among his descendants and their dispersion. During this period, the crown prince Oduduwa wanted to change the state religion to idolatry, so he turned the mosque into a temple for idol worship. He had a chief priest called Asara, who himself was an idol-maker. Asara had a son named Braima, who, as a child, detested his father's profession. He grew up to become a follower of Muhammad (the founder of Islam). While he helped his father sell some of the carved images, he wasn't a willing participant.

The town frequently went on three-day hunting expeditions to celebrate the gods. Braima used one of these occasions to destroy the gods in the temple since those that might oppose him were out of town. When the expedition party returned and discovered what Braima had done, he was ordered to be burned alive. This led to a war between the followers of the gods and the Muslims. The Muslims won the war, and Lamurudu was killed. His children and their sympathizers were driven out of Mecca. Oduduwa and his children escaped with two idols, and they journeyed eastward for ninety days until they reached Ife, where they settled. (Ife is another name for the aforementioned Ile-Ife.)

Considering their manners and customs, it is undeniable that the Yorubas migrated from the east; however, it is highly disputable that they originated from the Arabian region. Mecca has no record of them in its history books, and such an important event would not have gone unnoticed. However, these accounts sometimes do have a grain of truth in them, so it is possible that more may be uncovered as time passes.

After Oduduwa settled in Ife, he gave birth to a son named Okanbi. Okanbi had seven children who would later establish the different kingdoms that make up some of the Yoruba lands today. The names of the princes and princesses are Owu, Orangun, Popo, Sabe, Ketu, Oyo, and Benin. Oduduwa also had a grandson named

Oranyan, who would later establish one of the biggest Yoruba empires.

Despite all of these varying creation accounts, there is no doubt that the Yorubas regard Oduduwa as their founding and spiritual father.

# Origins of the Tribes

The Yoruba might be one large ethnic group, but there are many tribes within the culture that, in one way or another, can trace their origin to Oduduwa and the city of Ile-Ife. As said earlier, most of the major tribes sprang from Oduduwa's grandchildren. All of the other minor tribes originated from one of these seven tribes: Ketu, Owu, Sabe, Orangun, Ila, Popo, and Benin. When Oduduwa migrated from the east, there is a possibility that the eastern region contained natives who were conquered and absorbed into the culture. The Yoruba culture established and extended their kingdom as far as Ashanti, Ghana, because Oranyan and his brother were able to push their conquest in every direction.

*Map of Yorubaland*

## Oyo

Oranyan is known as the founder of the Oyo Empire. He was the youngest among the seven grandchildren of Oduduwa. Before he departed from Ife, Oranyan was already a distinguished and brave warrior. This is probably one of the reasons why he became successful in his conquests. According to one account, Oranyan agreed with his brother to attack a northern kingdom that had insulted his grandfather. Another version of the event said Oranyan left on an expedition to Mecca to avenge the death of his great-grandfather.

On the way, the two brothers quarreled and split up, going their separate ways. Oranyan wandered south to Bussa, where a chief there extended his hospitality. After explaining his predicament to the chief, Oranyan was given a charmed snake. As instructed, Oranyan followed the snake for seven days until it arrived at a spot and vanished into the ground. There, Oranyan established the Oyo Empire.

While the city was still under construction, they were constantly attacked by the Bariba of Borgu, who wanted to dominate the new city. At this point, the warrior Ajagunla (also known as Orangun, one of the legendary grandsons of Oduduwa) stepped in and helped the newly founded city win the war. Not long after this, Oranyan had a son named Ajuwon Ajaka. Much later, he gave birth to another son known as Shango.

Oranyan became the first Oba (ruler) of the Oyo Empire, and Shango, known as the Thunder God, became the third king. The empire no longer exists today, though there is still a ruler over the city of Odo who claims ancestry to Oranyan. The current Alaafin (emperor) of Oyo is Lamidi Olayiwola Adeyemi III.

## Ijebu

The Ijebus have different accounts of their origin. One version states they are descended from a victim who had been offered for sacrifice by the king of Benin to the god of the ocean. However, another account claims that the Ijebus are descended from Obanta, who was offered as a human sacrifice by the king of Owu. After being left for dead, he revived and crawled into a bush, where he survived on fruit before later dabbling in farming.

It is worth noting that in both accounts, the founders were victims of human sacrifice. Another account claims that Obanta led people out of Ile-Ife to form Ijebu-Ode. He led them until he reached old age, at which point he was instructed by Ifa (the chief god and the god of divination) to leave and die outside of the town.

The kings of the Ijebus are known as Awujale, and the current Awujale of the Ijebu Kingdom is Sikiru Kayode Adetona.

### Ondo

The killing of twins was a prevalent practice among the early Yoruba people. And somehow, this practice is what brought about the establishment of the Ondo Kingdom. One of the wives of the Oyo Empire birthed twins in an era when twins were considered an abomination. The Alaafin, Oluaso, was not happy about this and ordered them removed from the kingdom. The princess left with a number of friends and journeyed to the present site of Ondo, meaning "settler." One of the twins died at Epe, which was near Ondo. The other twin, Airo, would later become the Osemawe of Ondo. The current Osemawe is Dr. Victor A. Kiladejo.

### Egba

The Egba people established their homeland in the Egba forest after migrating from Oyo. Most families in Egba can trace their ancestry to Oyo, hence the popular saying, "Egbas who do not have Oyo roots must be slaves." This means that if they could not trace their roots, they must have belonged to the early Egba people, who were conquered by the settlers.

Over the centuries, the Egba people evolved from small hamlets to villages and are now cities, which operate independently. The first Alake of Egbaland was Okukenu Sagbua, and the current one is Adedotun Aremu Gbadebo III.

## Ekiti

The Ekiti people are among the original inhabitants of the country absorbed by Oduduwa when he migrated from Mecca. Ekiti means "mound," which is derived from the mountainous features of the area. The region has extensive vegetation and is well watered.

One account says the Ekiti people are descended from one of the offspring of Oduduwa. Olofin, one of Oduduwa's offspring, had sixteen children of his own. Olofin decided to venture from Ife in search of greener pastures. Olofin and his offspring journeyed until they reached flat terrain. Two of his children decided to stay behind while the rest of the family continued their journey until they reached a land with many hills. Thus, they named the place *Ile olokiti*, meaning the "land of hills." The Ekiti Kingdom was divided into several kingdoms over time. Today, Ekiti State is one of the states that comprises Nigeria.

## Ijesha

The Ijesha have different origin stories because their founder was different from the present-day people. The first account relates to the earliest Yoruba people when they had just migrated from the east and subdued the natives. At this time, human sacrifices were common, and slaves were often used as the victims. Slaves were captured from a district called Obokun and treated like cattle to be sacrificed to the gods. This prompted the name *Ije orisa*, meaning "foods for the gods."

Another account says the present-day Ijesha hailed from Ekiti. According to the customs back then, they were to go on a three-month hunting expedition for their king every year. On one such expedition, they found a region with plenty of game and an agreeable climate. The native Ijesha (probably a remnant of the former sacrificial victim) was peaceful. However, these people were quickly subdued by the invaders. One of their chiefs was spared due to his kind and gentle nature. He quickly rose through the ranks and eventually became the second-in-command to the chiefs of the invaders. The current Oba of Ijeshaland is Oba Gabriel Adekunle Aromolaranfall.

# Chapter 2 – The Development of the Early Yoruba Society

After the establishment of the early Yoruba kingdoms, the people began to advance in terms of civilization and structure. The Iron Age brought about a significant transformation, as it would stimulate a great advancement of culture. The Iron Age first came to Nigeria in early 700 BCE. According to archaeologists, the knowledge of ironworking might have arrived in West Africa through pot production.

The ironmaking process is a dangerous occupation that requires the use of a high amount of heat. Due to this, most iron-smelting centers were located far from residential areas, usually in the forest, where iron-bearing rock clay is readily available. This iron-bearing rock clay is heated to remove the iron from its ore, where it is cooled and sold to the blacksmith as iron ingots. The blacksmiths used the ingot to fabricate tools.

In the Yoruba culture, iron smelting and the fabrication of tools from iron is overseen by one of their deities known as Ogun (also known as Alakaaiye, meaning "the wielder of arms of working people"). Ogun is believed to be the god of iron and the patron of all working men. Iron-smelting workshops served as shrines to this deity, and sacrifices were rendered to the deity in the workshop. Blacksmiths were not the only ones that worshiped Ogun; it is believed that people using any form of metal in their daily activities (sculptors, farmers, woodworkers, hunters, etc.) offered sacrifices to this deity for good luck.

The discovery of iron was the second greatest discovery in West Africa after the discovery of agriculture. The Iron Age impacted the Yoruba culture positively, especially as it helped in the improvement of farming tools. Their first fabricated tools were crude at first but improved considerably with time. The improved tools made it possible to clear a large portion of land and dig and till the land for agricultural purposes. With more refined tools, more land became accessible for agriculture. Early Yoruba farmers learned quite early on the importance of leaving the ground fallow to retain soil fertility. The presence of more accessible land led to increased crop production, which eventually resulted in farmers developing methods of harvesting, storing, and protecting crops.

With an improved storage process, food became readily available, which led to a rise in the population in Yorubaland. The gradual increase in the population led to the emergence of settlements in more areas of the country. As the settlements increased, the forests separating the settlements from each other soon became open farmland.

The improvement and availability of tools gave rise to various professions and facilitated the division of labor. While farming was the main occupation of the Iron Age, some men became more involved in hunting due to greatly improved tools. From the onset, hunters were held in high regard. Apart from supplying the community with meat, other professions depended on them. For instance, potters and iron smelters depended on hunters to find good clay deposits. Also, the people relied on them to provide security against raiders and thieves and to help find clean brooks and streams. If there was a need for a group to relocate, the responsibility to find a new spot to settle and the best route to reach it usually fell on the hunters.

Another notable profession made possible by the Iron Age was the arts. Some of the earliest sculptures were done in terracotta. Also, the earliest wood carvings were made possible through the use of iron tools. Most of these carvings were used in house decorations as well as shrines.

As you can probably guess, the Iron Age had an impact on the economy. Iron tools improved the harvesting of oil palm trees, which was one of their major crops. The development of tools and skills helped the Yoruba farmers incorporate more crops into their farming. Among the many crops they planted was cotton, which opened up the weaving industry. The Yoruba also cultivated plants to use in dyeing cloths.

The coming of the Iron Age was a huge blessing, as it led to improved skills and better management of the environment. People learned how to build better and stronger homes, and this led to people erecting buildings that housed their extended families under the same roof. This birthed the concept of agbo-ile, a compound for the family that consisted of many homes with a number of courtyards around which the homes were positioned.

Architectural and aesthetic improvements to the agbo-ile turned it into a strong and safe haven. Plaster was used for the walls, which increased the safety and durability of the home. Also, weaving thatched roofs became an art, and the roofs would last for generations, with only the need for minor repairs. The agbo-ile gradually became a competition, with people trying to outdo each other in regard to decorations. These decorations also included shrines.

The rivalries between compounds resulted in artistic expressions like oriki. This is poetry in which each lineage glorifies itself and preserves its history. Facial markings also became a way to identify with one's ancestry. All of this contributed to the development of the

Yoruba people's identity and distinctiveness, especially when it came to lineages and settlements.

The growth and development of the Yoruba society started with the smallest unit: the family. The oldest living male member of the family was seen as the leader. He was the keeper of the family's customs, secrets, and totems (objects treasured and passed down by the leaders of the family/group). The leader was seen as the family's spiritual guide and the one who tended to the family shrine. What started as a closely knit family soon grew into a large group bound by shared beliefs, values, and rules. At some point, the leader of each settlement began wearing objects that helped indicate they were the leader.

There were different types of organizations in the earliest settlements. Still, the most common was the age grade, which was used to provide appropriate tasks for the people in the agbo-ile, like keeping an open space clean. Over time, the concept of the age grade evolved and began to include new rules and regulations. Apart from one's compound or lineage, the age grade was one of the most popular ways to identify oneself among the early Yoruba people.

Most adult men were farmers and were assisted by their wives and children. A typical day in the agbo-ile started at dawn, where most men went out to their farm. Those who were left behind included the elderly, children, and those with a home-based occupation. The homebound people carried out domestic activities while the children played under the watchful eyes of the aged and nursing mothers. By the late afternoon, the farmers would return home, bearing produce and firewood. Dinner would be served in the evening, and the hours after dinner were used for socializing. The men conversed while sharing a keg of palm wine while the women performed light domestic chores. The children listened and told stories, usually folklore.

The agbo-ile was one of the building blocks of the economy. Each agbo-ile took produce to the village market, and some agbo-iles became known for the things they sold. One of the earliest modes of trade was bartering, although the Yoruba later used cowry shells as a form of payment.

One of the triumphs of the early Yoruba people was the development of traditional medicine. Over the centuries, each settlement accumulated knowledge of various herbs to treat illnesses. They also gained vast knowledge on the nature of different diseases. Each settlement had a professional herbalist that the people depended on for treatment. Over time, professional herbalists evolved into specialists, i.e., those specializing in treating mental diseases, delivery of babies, etc. Over the years, the settlements set up rules and regulations in regard to herbalists.

The birth of a baby was celebrated in the agbo-ile. For several weeks, the older women within the compound served as the baby's mother in what is called collective nurturing. They also helped the new mother by passing on their knowledge to her.

Children, both living and those yet unborn, were regarded as important members of the compound. It is believed that everything a lineage owned belonged to the next generation. This shows that the early Yorubas valued their children and invested heavily in their training and education. The next generation's education was a collective effort, and each agbo-ile raised their young in its image, with the people passing down their knowledge of their ancestral history. They also trained their young in their lineage's profession. For instance, some agbo-ile were known for a particular trade, and the people of the compound would often continue practicing it in the next generation.

Births were not the only celebrations in the agbo-ile. There were also village and lineage festivals, weddings, and funerals. The Yorubas celebrated weddings in a grand style. They involved three major activities: the introduction ceremony, the betrothal ceremony, and the ceremonial journey of the bride back to her husband's agbo-ile. Nowadays, the Yoruba people call their wedding celebrations *owambe* and have simplified the ceremonies into just two: the introduction and the engagement.

The Yorubas believed in exogamy, which means marriages often occurred outside of one's family and clan. The Yorubas also practiced a patrilineal kinship system, whereby every child belonged to their father's lineage and could only inherit from that lineage. A woman married into a family from another compound automatically became her husband's family and could never revert to her father's family, even after her death.

Mourning was another event done collectively in the agbo-ile. Mourning could go on for days, especially if it was the death of a young adult. In the early days, most children died in infancy, and few made it to adulthood. The people always buried their dead in their compound.

Overall, the agbo-ile was one of the most important factors in the development of the early Yoruba civilization. Each agbo-ile had a system of government under the leadership of the olori-ebi, who acted as the ruler and the priest. Each village or settlement had a government with an exalted ruler, chiefs, rules, and laws guiding them.

Disputes and quarrels were settled by the olori-ebi (the oldest man in the village or compound), but he had the help of the elders. They exercised judicial and penal authority in all matters concerning the lineage. One of the olori-ebi's duties was to make room for members of the lineage to express their opinions.

The earliest Yorubas had a distinct religion, and they followed the religious guidance of the oldest member of the family. Also, as more occupations were established, patron gods and goddesses began to appear. Farmers, hunters, and market women all had a god or goddess attached to their profession. Deities were accepted and worshiped in Yorubaland. The number of deities worshiped varied according to each settlement.

The Yoruba believed that all existence could be found in two realms: the lower realm and the upper realm. The upper realm consists of two spheres: a higher and a lower. The higher is overseen by Olodumare, the creator of all things. The second sphere, the one closer to humans, is the home to gods like Ifa, Ogun, and Obatala. Divination, the ability to tell the future, was an important part of the Yoruba culture. It was made possible through Ifa.

Another development in the Yoruba culture was the belief in the afterlife. The Yorubas believed that people who died went on to live in another realm. This explains why their dead were buried with articles of clothing. The root of their belief in the afterlife began with their idea that each individual has a minimum of three spiritual beings living within them. The first spirit, *emi*, resides in the heart and lungs and is powered by the winds entering the nostrils, the same way fire is powered by the wind produced by a blacksmith's bellows. The word *emi* can be translated as either "life" or "breath" because, without life, there is no breath. And without breath, there is no life. It is with *emi* that a man moves, walks, eats, speaks, sees, hears, and makes love.

The second spiritual being is *ojiji*, which means "shadow." Every individual is followed by their shadow throughout their life, and when he or she dies, the shadow also follows them to their final destination in the afterlife. The third being is called *eleda*, meaning "spirit." The *eleda* is regarded as the guardian soul of an individual, and it requires regular sacrifices to continue serving the individual.

These are the basic spiritual beings that all individuals must have to live. The other types of spiritual beings can be acquired at birth or over the course of one's lifetime by making agreements with the gods in charge of those beings. At death, these spiritual beings evacuate the body of the individual and await his or her presence in the afterlife. Apart from the beings, the individual is also welcomed by their family members who had already died.

A person's afterlife depended on the deeds they had done during their life. After dying, the *eleda* reports the person's earthly deeds to Olorun (the ruler of the heavens). The good souls are sent to Orun Rere ("Good Heaven"), and the wicked souls who are guilty of witchcraft, theft, or murder are sent to Orun Buburu ("Wicked Heaven") or Orun Apadi ("Hell Fire") as punishment.

Even though the missionaries introduced science and the Christian belief of the afterlife, there are still Yorubas who believe in the concept of having a guardian soul, *eleda*, that is in charge of their destiny; a shadow, *ojiji*, that follows them through life recording their actions; and an *emi* that gives them breath to live. There are about one hundred million practitioners of the Yoruba faith today.

Another popular belief in Yorubaland was (and still is) reincarnation. They believed that the dead would be reincarnated into one of their descendants, which is a belief that has influenced many Yoruba names. For instance, the name Babatunde is given to a male child whose grandfather died close to his birth, while Yetunde or Iyabo is given to a female child whose grandmother had passed away recently. The name Babatunde means "father has returned," and Yetunde or Iyabo translates to "mother has returned."

There is also the concept of akudaaya, which roughly translates to "death without leaving earth." This is similar to the concept of ghosts in other cultures. The difference is that the ghosts in Yorubaland go on to live new lives. They start new families and may possibly live until they die of old age. Not everyone who dies becomes an akudaaya, but if a person dies a wrongful death or before their predestined time of death, the chance of becoming one increases. After death, the person's soul leaves their body, travels to another village or town, and goes on living until their predestined time of death. The people in the new town are able to see and touch the individual, which means they view the akudaaya as just another person. However, the moment a single person becomes aware, the akudaaya flees and moves to another place to start all over. This is another belief that is still prevalent in present-day Yorubaland.

# Chapter 3 – Deified Yoruba Heroes

The ancient Yoruba heroes were not just heroes; they were also kings turned gods, goddesses, and deities. The origin story of the Yorubas cannot be told without speaking of them. They were so revered that each of them had a dedicated group of people, agbo-ile, and villages that worshiped them. Before Britain colonized Nigeria, which brought about a massive missionary campaign, the primary religion of the Yorubas was idol worship. Some of their gods were Oduduwa, Shango, Ogun, Oya, and Oshun, although there were many, many more. These heroes are still worshiped today, but idol worship is now the minority among the Yorubas, with many people identifying as Christians or Muslims.

## Oduduwa (Odùduwà)

It is only befitting that the first god to be discussed is Oduduwa, as he is one of the heroes who cannot be left out when discussing the Yorubas. Oduduwa was coined from the name *Odu ti o da Iwa*, meaning the "author of existence." Yoruba historians have stated that Oduduwa was the son of Olodumare. You might recall that Oduduwa was sent to earth via a chain; this earned him the name Atenworo, meaning "one who descends from a chain."

In the early days, Ile-Ife had close to thirteen communities, and each community had its own Oba (ruler or king). Oduduwa was popular among most of these communities, and this allowed him to overthrow Obatala, his brother, from the throne and take over. It also led to hostilities between Oduduwa and Obatala, the latter of whom had (according to some versions of the legend) founded Ile-Ife on orders from Olodumare, the supreme god.

Oduduwa changed the decentralized system of Ile-Ife to a centralized one and created the title of Ooni of Ife. Previously, there were thirteen Obas, but with Oduduwa's new title, there was only one ruler of Ife: Oduduwa.

Oduduwa lived a fulfilling life with a large family. He had multiple wives: Omonide (his favorite) and Adetinrin Anasin. He also had many children, including Orunto, Iyunade, Ajagunla, and Ifagbamila, just to name a few.

After Oduduwa's peaceful death, the Yorubas started to worship him. Human sacrifices were offered to him until the time of the British protectorate.

### Ogun (Ògún)

Ogun was the Ooni of Ife after Oduduwa. He was skilled in metalwork, which earned him the title god of iron after his death. Ogun's expertise in hunting made people call him Osin-Imole, which means "chief among the divinities."

According to Ife mythology, when the other gods came to earth, Ogun cleared the path for them with a metal ax and had a dog as his companion. Ogun loved being alone on the hilltop, but when he was tired of his lonely life, he came down the hill, clothed in fire and blood. He wanted to mingle with the people, so he took fronds from a palm tree and went to Ire, where he was crowned king.

Ogun's death is interesting. His subjects refused to pay him the respect he wanted, so he killed them and then killed himself. But he wasn't buried. He disappeared into the earth, but he told his people that whenever they called him, he would answer.

Some parts of Yorubaland still offer sacrifices to Ogun. The main items used for sacrifice are iron and dogs because of his love for hunting and dogs.

### Oranyan (Ọranyan)

Oranyan, also called Oranmiyan, was the grandson of Oduduwa and the son of Ogun. A peculiar fact about him is that he was birthed after his mother had an affair with both Ogun and Oduduwa; thus, he is known as the "man of two fathers."

His skin tone carved out his name. He was mostly light-skinned like his father, Ogun, but he was dark-skinned in some parts like his grandfather, Oduduwa. This led to the creation of the name Oranmiyan (*Oran ni omo ni yan*), meaning, "the child has chosen to be controversial."

Oranyan was brave and a great hunter. At that time, Ile-Ife had no military, so he took it upon himself to defend it. This made him the first Akogun (general) of Ife.

During one of the earliest wars, Obalufon Ogbogbodirin, the fourth Ooni of Ife, sent Oranyan off with his brother to conquer Igodomigodo (the historical name of the Benin Empire). Obalufon's aim was for Oranyan to die since Oranyan was giving him trouble.

Unfortunately for Obalufon, Oranyan didn't die; he actually won the war. But he didn't go back to Ife; instead, he stayed at Igodomigodo. However, he noticed that the people of Igodomigodo didn't like him. This made him uncomfortable, and he felt it was wrong to rule them when he wasn't from their land, so he left.

Before he left, he took the daughter of Egor's chief as his wife, and they had a child together named Eweka. Egor was located nearby, and the people accepted Eweka more willingly. He became the first Oba of Benin. (Some sources that Oranyan was the first ruler of Benin, who then passed the throne to his son so he could continue his explorations.)

Oranyan moved northward with his large army. Eventually, he found a secure place where he established the Oyo Empire, calling it Oyo-Ile. After conquering a nearby village, he took another wife.

Oranyan was a great traveler and explored many different places. After his adventures, he went back to Ile-Ife and demanded that the throne be handed to him, despite being Ogun's youngest son. Because Oranyan was a warrior and highly feared, the fifth Ooni of Ife stepped down so he could take over. He ruled for a short while, but eventually, he wanted to continue his adventure. So, he left the village. But before leaving, he told the people of Ile-Ife that if they needed him to protect them, they should make some incantations to summon him. He assured them that he would come to save them.

There was peace in Ile-Ife until Oranyan's enemies attacked the city. The people called out to Oranyan with the proper incantations, and he came back to fight for them. But while killing his enemies, he mistakenly killed some of his people, including his best friend. This left him devastated. Agonized by what he had done, he drove his staff into the ground and left on his horse. The Yorubas never saw him again.

Oranyan was a great warrior who successfully ruled two (possibly three) Yoruba kingdoms and established the Oyo Empire. The staff he left behind is now known as the Staff of Oranyan, and it is a tourist attraction that brings people from all over the world to Ile-Ife.

### Ajaka

Ajaka, the son of Oranyan, was the only legendary king to reign the Oyo Empire twice, as he was removed from office and then called back to reclaim the throne. Even though warfare was the order of the day, Ajaka was a man of peace. Due to his calm nature, he was made to step down to allow his fierce brother, Shango, to rule.

After Shango's death, Ajaka was called back to reclaim the throne, but his rule must have surprised the people. He had changed a lot during the years, and he had become even fiercer than Shango. He killed the maternal relations of Shango with arrows mounted on birds. He waged war with literally everybody, including over one thousand of his chiefs and princes.

Ajaka had special people called medicine men who made charms for him. After the war, the medicine men requested to return to their homes, but Ajaka refused. He was afraid that other kings would request their services and that they would get charms as well. Seeing that Ajaka was not ready to let them go, the medicine men all vanished except for one, Elenre. Ajaka was furious, and he took his anger out on Elenre.

Ajaka attempted to kill Elenre, but all his attempts were futile until Ijaehin, Elenre's wife, told Ajaka what to do. Ijaehin told him to pull some grass from Elenre's roof to make him powerless. Another version of the story claims that it was Omoloja, one of Ajaka's maids who was sleeping with Elenre, who told Ajaka to decapitate Elenre with a sharp palm leaf blade.

Ajaka's men followed the directives provided by the snitch and then cut off Elenre's head. His head fell into Ajaka's hands, who caught it unconsciously. The head became stuck to his hand, and all attempts to take it off were worthless. This drained Ajaka because the head ate every food and drank brought to him. Ajaka was dying, and many magicians were called to neutralize the charm. Only one was able to succeed: Asawo.

When Asawo entered Ajaka's chambers, he prostrated himself before Elenre's head and explained that he had no other choice but to come because it was the king's request. By doing this, Asawo emphasized how powerful Elenre was, and he praised him for all his magic works and how he had defeated a lot of people.

Elenre was pleased with this and rolled off Ajaka's hand to form a river at Oyo called Odo Elenre ("Elenre's river"). His wife, Ijaehin, also formed a river at Oyo, but Elenre ordered the river to remain stagnant. The head incident caused Ajaka to make a rule that no king would be present at an execution in the future. There is no record of what happened to Ajaka after this event.

### Shango (Sàngó)

Shango is the most popular orisha, which is a spirit known to interact with humans. Shango, also called Jakuta, was the second son of Oranyan. He was wild and had a fiery temper.

Shango's brother Ajaka was the ruler of the Oyo Empire before Shango came to power. The Olowu (the ruler) of the Owu Kingdom and Ajaka's cousin constantly intimidated Ajaka, making him appear less powerful to the people. The Olowu once forced Ajaka to pay tribute to him, despite the fact that Ajaka was also a king. This led to Ajaka's removal from the throne. Shango then took over, and when the Olowu asked Shango to pay tribute to him, Shango refused. This caused a fight, during which Shango made the Olowu and his army fear him by emitting smoke and fire from his mouth. They never bothered him again.

One day, Shango desired to worship at his mother's burial ground, but he was unable to because he didn't remember her name. His mother, the daughter of Elempe, a Nupe king, died when he was an infant. To obtain her name, Shango commissioned a Tetu (king executioner) and a Hausa slave. (There are varying accounts on the number and type of people he sent to Nupe.) They were to travel to the land of the Nupe, specifically where his mother was from, to offer the sacrifice of a cow and a horse for his mother. Their mission was to listen for his mother's name when the sacrifice was being offered.

Upon reaching the town, King Elempe entertained the men sent by his grandson and offered them drinks and food. The Hausa slave got drunk, but the Tetu was very careful and avoided drinking. When the sacrifice started, only the Tetu paid attention and heard Shango's mother's name when it was mentioned.

When the men returned to Oyo, the Tetu was rewarded with money since he knew the name of Shango's mother. The Hausa slave was punished. He was given 122 razor cuts for failing to follow Shango's instructions. When the cuts had healed, the women in the palace, including Shango's wives, thought they were beautiful. They told this to Shango, leading him to make a rule that every royal should bear these cuts. Being one of the royals, Shango handed himself over to the markers to cut him with the razor, but he could only bear two cuts on his arm. However, this gave him an idea.

Oko was a very powerful region, as it bore the central seat of the government. Shango wanted to bring this seat to Oyo, but he knew that the prince at Oko would refuse. So, he devised a strategy to use the Hausa slave's cuts to achieve his goal.

He sent the Hausa slave and the markers to the prince at Oko. They had to convince the royals of the beauty of these cuts. The royals saw the slave and believed that the marks would look good on them as well. The markers made the cuts on them while they performed some rites. On the third day, Shango attacked Oko and overtook it because the royals were too weak to fight. He transferred the seat of government from Oko to Oyo, just as he wanted.

Shango reigned for seven years, during which he made conquests and showed his strength. He also made charms. There was a particular one that he made that caused lightning. One day, he wanted to try a new experiment. He ascended Ajaka hill with his slaves and cousins, intending to try out this new idea of creating a storm with the charm. Although he thought the idea to be useless, it actually worked—a little too well, in fact. The charm started a storm, and lightning struck the palace, igniting a fire. Before they could descend the hill to quench the fire, many of Shango's wives and children had already died.

Seeing that Shango was the reason behind the whole misfortune, he was made to renounce his throne. He was then brought to the court of his grandfather, Elempe, King of the Nupes. Not all of his people were against him, though; some wanted a peaceful resolution to the matter, and they offered to help him find wives who could bear him children. But because Shango couldn't stand having even a single person being against him, he left Oyo with some followers, including his head slave and favorite servant, Biri.

However, Biri didn't like Shango's decision and encouraged Shango to turn back and start a new life with the wives that had been offered to him. Shango refused, and Biri left him. The other followers followed in Biri's footsteps. Shango was left alone, which devasted him further, resulting in him hanging himself on a shea tree.

His friends heard of his death, and they paid homage by burning his body and burying the remains under the same tree before also committing suicide one by one. Biri was the first to commit suicide, and he was followed by other slaves and some of Shango's cousins. The deaths ended with Shango's favorite wife, Oya.

Some say Shango didn't commit suicide but entered into the ground and disappeared. Another claim is that he transformed into an orisha by ascending to heaven on a chain. Shango is still worshiped in some parts of Yorubaland as the god of lightning and thunder.

### Oshun (Ọṣun)

Oshun (also spelled as Osun) is another orisha. She is a river deity that represents femininity, fertility, and love. She was one of King Shango's wives. According to legend, she was sent to help Shango as an Irunmole, a spirit. It is said that the other Irunmoles sent to help the founding heroes create the world ignored Oshun and only started to respect her after Shango stood up for her.

There are two accounts of this story. One version claims that the female spirits sent to create the world wanted to be in control, but all their attempts were in vain because they lacked male approval.

Another account asserts that the male Irunmoles wanted to create a world free from female influence. However, doing this caused the world to fail. The first version is probably a patriarchal interpretation of the second story, which is more in line with the reverence of feminine power by traditional orisha worshipers. Even though the versions contradict each other, they both end the same way, with Shango telling the spirits to respect Oshun the way they respected him.

She is celebrated at the Osun-Osogbo festival, which is named after a sacred grove near the Osun River. It is held annually every August for two weeks. The festival started seven hundred years ago after Oshun revealed herself to a hunter named Olutimehin and his followers when they settled at the bank of the Osun River to survive the famine that had driven them from their former settlement. Oshun instructed the people to move up the river to higher ground and promised them prosperity if they offered her an annual sacrifice. The place the people moved to is now known as the city of Osogbo, and the sacrifice is still offered to her annually. However, the Osun-Osogbo festival is now more than just offering sacrifices. It is recognized as an international event, as it attracts worshipers and tourists from all over the world. The festival receives visitors from countries such as Brazil, Trinidad, Cuba, Jamaica, Tobago, Spain, the United States, and Canada.

### Oya

Oya was the youngest wife of Shango. Her powers were rooted in the natural world, and she controlled lightning, thunder, rainstorms, tornadoes, and hurricanes. What made her stand out amongst the other goddesses was her ability to relate with other women. Although she was a loving and caring mother, she could also transform into a fierce warrior in an instant.

Oya is venerated around the world. Some know her to be the guardian of the realms of life and death. Hence, she controlled activities related to death like funerals and spiritual communication, as well as reincarnation and psychic abilities. Her ability to call out or drive away the spirit of death made people fear her. Since Oya was the goddess of the wind, she gives the first breath humans take, but she also takes their last breath.

As the goddess of rain, Oya gave her husband the power to create storms, so storms followed whenever she and her husband walked together. This could be anything from gentle to violent rainstorms capable of bringing down strong buildings.

Oya met her husband in a forest. He came to kill a buffalo that he had been stalking for some time. Before he could strike a blow, the buffalo suddenly turned into a woman. He took her home, named her Oya, and then married her. Oya and Shango loved each other to the point that Oya followed Shango on his conquests. And when Shango died, Oya was so sad that she hid among a sheep flock to avoid being found before gathering the courage to join her husband in death (or disappearance, as some accounts say). This action makes her worshipers avoid eating sheep meat.

Oya sometimes changed to a buffalo, and when she left the earth, she pulled one of her horns out and gave it to her children. Every year, people offer buffalo horns to the shrines of Oya so that she may continue guiding them and bless them with favors. These people are called the "Children of Buffalo."

### Aganju

Aganju is another orisha, and he is associated with the sun and volcanoes. It is not known if the real Aganju has any connection to the mythical one. Some historians believe it might just be a coincidence that the two shared the same name.

Regardless, Aganju, the ruler of Oyo, was brave, and during his reign, he built houses and improved the lives of the people. His reign was prosperous until he fell in love with the daughter of another king. He waged war with this king for not allowing him to marry his daughter. The war claimed many lives, and during the war, Aganju killed his heir, Lugbe, because he caught him having an affair with Iyayun, his wife. Aganju suffered for years due to what he had felt forced to do, and he eventually died of grief.

Aganju's exact relationship with Shango is unclear, but there appears to be some sort of relationship between them. Some say that Aganju was the father of Shango, while others say that they were brothers.

# Chapter 4 – The Kingdoms of Yorubaland

There were many founding kingdoms in Yorubaland; however, not all are going to be mentioned in this chapter, as those other kingdoms are discussed extensively in other chapters. The Yoruba kingdoms are best divided into three geographical regions to better understand how each kingdom was established and flourished. These divisions are the central, southern, and eastern kingdoms.

*Map of major Yoruba cities*

# The Central Kingdoms

Territories in the central kingdoms include the Ife, Ilesha, Ifewara, and Owu kingdoms.

### The Ifewara Kingdom

Ifewara was founded almost a century after the establishment of Ile-Ife. It was situated toward the southeast of the prominent Ife Kingdom by Prince Olojo Agbele. Olojo Agbele had failed to secure the throne of Ile-Ife, so he left with his followers to a settlement not too far from Ife. The people in the settlement received him warmly and joined his followers to crown him as king. The new king called the new town Ifewara, meaning "Ife that is full of milk and honey."

Most of the beliefs and traditions that were practiced in Ile-Ife were replicated in Ifewara. For instance, both kingdoms had chiefs bearing the same titles, such as Obalufe and Obajio, and the same functions and respect were accorded to these chiefs precisely as it was done in Ife. Also, deities and celebrations were performed in the same manner. Ifewara was basically a smaller replica of Ile-Ife.

The people of Ifewara sought to be more recognized and come out of the shadow of their more prominent neighbor, so they demanded to have their kings wear a beaded crown. This was rejected by the Ooni of Ife in 1916. Ifewara strengthened its relationship with Ilesha; soon enough, they became independent of Ife. They asked the Owa of Ilesha to grant them permission to use a beaded crown. The Owa granted the request in 1946; however, the citizens of Ifewara protested against their ruler, claiming they were not under Ilesha rule either. By asking for permission, the people saw their king acting as subservient to the Owa.

### The Ilesha Kingdom (Ijesha Kingdom)

Most Yoruba kingdoms believe they originated from Ife. The Ijeshas (who populated the Ilesha Kingdom) are not exempted from this group. The Ijeshas had many cities, such as Ilesha, Otan, Ipetu

Jesa, Esa-Oke, and Imesi-Ile, which are generally found toward Ife's east. Ilesha was more prominent than the others.

Like most Yoruba kingdoms, an Ife prince by the name of Ajibogun established Ijeshaland after his journey to the coast to get some seawater, which had been recommended for Oduduwa's eye defects. According to tradition, Oduduwa was Ajibogun's grandfather. This quest was not easy, and Oduduwa feared that his grandson might never return, so he gave his remaining male heirs gifts and tokens to start their own kingdoms away from Ife. However, Ajibogun was still alive, and upon his return from the coast with the seawater, Oduduwa, grateful for his grandson's successful quest, gave him his sword known as Ida Ajase, meaning "sword of victory," as a token. Ajibogun took the sword and headed east toward the Ijesha forest with his followers. They settled in Igbadaiye; some scholars believe Ajibogun died there.

There are other versions of Ajibogun's story. Others say he became involved in conquests. He stayed in Ilemure, which he gave to his son Ooyela. This town was eventually named Ilu Obokun (Obukon is another name that is used in place of Ajibogun in the stories), and today, it is known as Ibokun.

The spirit of conquest continued for some time. The kings ruled Oke-Osun, Iwori, Ipole, and Ejioro before finally settling in Ilesha, with their king now called an Owa. During their journey to Ilesha, the conquerors encountered other settlements like Akogun, Ibosirin, Igbogi, Lurere, Asore, and Okesa, which collectively agreed to acknowledge the Owa as their king.

The Owa met a farmer in Okesa who grew okra (ila), a staple food for the king and his entourage. The title of Obanla (king of Okra-ila) was given to the farmer. Obanla became one of the highest titles in Ilesha, and he was the second in command to the Owa.

Another important position in the Ilesha Kingdom was the Ogboni of Obokun. The title was given to the ruler of Obokun before the Owa left for Ilesha. The Obokun had a shrine that had to be visited before a new Owa could be installed. There, rituals would be performed, likely blessing the king with a prosperous reign. This was done to pay homage to the fact that the people of Ilesha can trace themselves to Obokun.

# The Eastern Kingdoms

The Yoruba kingdoms moved eastward, beyond the hills and forests of Ilesha. These are the Ekiti and Akoko kingdoms. The Ekiti people have many small kingdoms identified in their history, like Ado, Ikole, Ijero, Ikere, Otun, Efon, Ogotun, Ire, and Obo. The prominent ones of historical significance are discussed in this chapter.

### The Ire Kingdom

This kingdom gained prominence in Yoruba history as the original home of Ogun, the god of iron. The first ruler of Ire, the Onire, was a high priest of Ogun, and the people believed that they evolved from him. Some Yoruba traditions confirm the Ire people originated from Ogun.

Ire was believed to be very powerful, so when some of the kingdoms were subduing other settlements and merging towns, they left Ire alone. This brought peace, stability, and prosperity to the kingdom at a time when migration and conquests were a common occurrence.

### The Ado Kingdom

Immigrant princes who were either denied the throne or left their home kingdom to establish their own communities founded most of the Yoruba kingdoms. Ado was one of the kingdoms established this way.

The founder was an Ife prince known as Awamaro, meaning the "restless one," and he had the title of Ewi, meaning the "speaker." Awamaro left Ife with his brother Oranyan (yes, the famous ruler mentioned above) to Benin. After some years of living there, Awamaro left Oranyan in Benin and journeyed north with his followers. Due to his restlessness, he also journeyed east as far as the

Ekiti forests. He was urged to stop at Agbado by the older people in his group. They knew they could not continue on with Awamaro, so this group chose to settle in Agbado.

Relentless in his journey, Awamaro continued east until he arrived at a settlement surrounding the spiritual Olota Rock. The power of the rock was thought to be controlled by the Elesun of Ilesun; the Elesun was the chief priest and also the protector of the area by the Olota Rock.

After arriving in Ilesun, Awamaro and his followers settled and lived with the people there peacefully until clashes erupted between them. During the fighting, Awamaro subdued his opponent, the Elesun, and cut off his head before establishing the Ado Kingdom and taking the title Ewi of Ado. The Elesun's influence in Ado is still seen today, with each succeeding Ewi paying obeisance at the Elesun's grave before assuming the throne.

The leaders in Awamaro's group and those of the older settlement became the chiefs of the Ado Kingdom. Centuries later, the people of Ila also joined the Ado Kingdom. The leader of Ila, known as the Alarierin, was later made a chief in the Ado Kingdom. The people of Ila were originally from the Ila Orangun Kingdom formed by one of the male descendants of Oduduwa. It was part of the first seven kingdoms established by the Oduduwa bloodline that departed from Ife.

### The Ikere Kingdom

The Ikere Kingdom was known to have challenges with its leadership. By the late 17th century, the challenges brought an internal change in the leadership structure of the Ikere Kingdom. Like other established kingdoms, the creator of Ikere migrated from Ife but was later dethroned by a trusted friend, Ogoga, who was a famous Edo hunter living in Ikere.

The Olukere, besides being the king of Ikere, was also the priest of the Olosunta Rock; Olosunta was regarded as the highest deity in the land. The Olukere was in charge of the rituals at the shrine, and due to his busy schedule, he was said to have instructed Ogoga to help attend to administrative issues like judging disputes between the townspeople. This led to the usurpation of the Olukere's power and authority, although how Ogoga did this is not clearly understood. Ogoga became the king while the ousted Olukere became the high priest of the kingdom.

### The Akure Kingdom

The princes from Ife always moved out of the kingdom to establish a new settlement. This was the case with Akure, which was established by Omoremilekun Asodeboyede, an Ife prince. Asodeboyede wandered around the forests of Efon and Ara before settling in Akure.

Akure was founded along the route going from Ife to modern-day Edo State. Asodeboyede conquered all of the nearby settlements, such as Oke-Aro, Idopetu, Obanla, Ijomu, and Ilemo. He combined these settlements and established his new kingdom in the most fertile and productive part of the forest.

Akure received its name from a historical event that occurred during that period. When Asodeboyede got to this location, the array of royal beads around his neck suddenly came loose. This led to his follower exclaiming, "Akun re!" meaning "The beads have snapped!" Thus, the settlement was named Akun re, and over time, it changed into Akure.

Deji is the official title of the Akure kings, but initially, they were called Ajapada. This title came about when Oba Olofinleyo married the daughter of the Oba of Ijeshaland. The princess gave birth to a son while her father was still on a pilgrimage. When he returned, he gifted the baby a small diadem. This act gave the child his praise name, which is found in oriki (praise poetry). The young boy was named Owafadeji, meaning "Owa gifted him a diadem." This name would stick with him until adulthood. By the time he became a king, the praise name had become the title of those who ruled Akure, as subsequent kings would later take Deji as their official title. However, even today, Ajapada remains a part of the Deji's ceremonial title.

The king's palace was built in 1150 CE in the center of the town. Akure was mostly independent throughout its history; however, at one point, they were subject to other kingdoms like the Kingdom of Benin and paid tribute to them. Benin used the Akure Kingdom as a base for trading, and subsequent Akure rebellions were put down. In the early 19th century, Akure briefly gained its independence from Benin rule, but it was conquered once more. The Deji was killed for his participation in the rebellion.

Akure and other Ekiti towns also became subject to Ibadan, a city located in southwestern Nigeria, in 1854. Akure endured Ibadan rule for about twenty years; in 1876, the Akure Kingdom rebelled and received its freedom during the following war between the principal Yoruba states.

## Akoko Kingdoms

The Akoko countryside had hills similar to Ekiti, but they were more rugged. Unlike the Ekiti, whose settlers came from Ile-Ife, history revealed that the Akoko region had settlers who did not speak Yoruba. There was a different mix of people, with the Edo, Yoruba, Afenmai, and Nupe coming together to trade or try to establish settlements.

The Akoko area was provided natural defenses by the hilly countryside. The region frequently saw military campaigns from its neighbors like the Edo, Nupe, and Owo people, so the region could not boast of kingdoms as big and prosperous as the Ekiti countryside.

The kingdoms established in Akoko follow the same trend as most of the other Yoruba towns, with people migrating from another place. The princes of Benin who lost the throne or who enjoyed exploring often came to this region to conquer and establish new kingdoms.

Many towns in Akoko, like Ishua, Ipe, Arigidi, Ifira, Ipesi, Afa, and Epeme, can connect their foundation to the Kingdom of Benin.

Most of these kingdoms, in the earlier stages of their history, did not operate a monarchy form of government like the Yoruba, but due to the constant displacement of people because of military campaigns, they adopted the Yoruba monarchy structure. During the prolonged war between the Yoruba principal states, Akoko, unlike the Ekiti people, did not experience most of the war since its rugged terrain acted as a natural defense against the Ibadan cavalry coming from the south. In addition, the bravery of the Akoko people helped to protect most of the towns.

# The Southern Kingdoms

These kingdoms occupied territories closer to the Atlantic coast, and the regions were covered with thick forests. The kingdoms found here are Ilaje, Ikale, Ondo, Ijebu, Awori, Itsekiri, and Owo.

### The Owo Kingdom

Owo was founded by an Ife prince named Asunlola Ojugbelu (also known as Omolaghaye). He was one of Orunmila's sons. (Orunmila was an orisha responsible for knowledge, divination, and wisdom.)

History revealed that Ojugbelu left Ife around the 12th century. Ojugbelu and his followers did not take the expected route but went through Idanre, where they stopped in places like Uji and Upafa. However, the group could not establish their kingdom in this location for several reasons, such as bad weather, extreme hostility from prior settlers, difficult terrain, and the lack of food and water. They tried again in another location called Ugbo Ogwata, but it also didn't work out. Eventually, though, they got to an old route that stretched from Ife to Benin. They decided to establish their kingdom, Owo, along this route. However, it was Imade, the son of Ojugbelu, who brought the group to this spot because Ojugbelu had died in Upafa.

Upon arriving at this location, they met settlements that were already established. These settlements include Okese, Omu, Oko, Efene, Ilale, Utelu, Igbe, and Idasen. The group led by Imade founded three early settlements, but they were often overcome. The Olomu of Omu chased Imade and his followers from the area. Efene, which was ruled by the Elefene, was the strongest of the three settlements, and it also repelled the newcomers. Idasen was one of the few settlements that received the migrants peacefully; however, adversity arose there when the migrants tried to assert authority over the other settlements, which led to hostilities.

Imade and his group were still able to establish their new kingdom amidst all the conflicts. The three aforementioned settlements attempted to unify other settlements against Imade. This prolonged fighting went on for many generations, and eventually, some settlements were overcome. Those who were friends with the new kingdom merged with it, with their leaders becoming chiefs. Owo grew and expanded slowly while later absorbing all the other settlements. They were forced to acknowledge the authority of the Olowu of Owo as their leader. Each settlement had its quarters controlled by their former leaders, who were now chiefs in the larger Owo Kingdom.

### The Ode-Itsekiri Kingdom

This kingdom was established along some of the coastal lagoons, although there are reservations about how they got to this area and the origins of their monarchy. It is assumed that a Yoruba sub-group went as far as this region during the general expansion of the Yoruba people. However, their traditions are closely related to that of the Edo people.

Their origin can be traced to a Benin prince called Iginuwa. After he lost the throne to other competitors, he journeyed to the western delta. He met some Yoruba people who had already settled there. These earlier settlers accepted Iginuwa as their king, but the reason for this is actually not known. Many theories have sprung up over the years, with one being that Iginuwa impressed the established settlers with his royal regalia. It is also possible that the bilingualism of the Benin court played a major factor. Iginuwa might have spoken both Edo and Yoruba, making it easier for the Yoruba settlers to accept him.

The kingdom was quite diverse, absorbing the Edo, Ijaw, and Urhobo languages and cultural elements. Nevertheless, Yoruba remained its main language, which shows the dominance of the Yoruba people in the area before the arrival of Iginuwa. The capital of the new kingdom was called Ode-Itsekiri, which was similar to what the neighboring Yoruba kingdoms, like Ilaje and Ikale, called their towns.

### The Ilaje Kingdom

The Ilaje group created their settlements along the coast, sharing borders with the coastal Ijebu people. They were also the closest Yoruba neighbors of the Itsekiri people. They occupied lagoons and creeks, which made the conglomeration of their population in a particular location largely impossible. However, they still had some kind of monarchy in place.

During the general Yoruba expansion, the Ilaje people created two kingdoms: a western kingdom with its capital in Mahin and an eastern kingdom with its capital in Ugbo. It is thought that the Ugbo Kingdom was the older of the two.

The economy of the Ilaje people was based on fishing and trading since they lived, for the most part, around water. The worship of water deities and other Yoruba gods was deeply rooted in their culture. According to tradition, these spirits were usually involved in disputes over fishing rights, trade, accusations of stealing, and many other things. The most prominent among these spiritual deities was Ayelala, and the most popular shrine of hers was found along the Oluwa River. She is still widely feared among the Ilaje communities today because of her severe punishments of dishonesty.

## The Ikale Kingdom

The Ikales shared a boundary with the Ilajes along the coast, but southward, the land was mostly thick forests divided by water bodies. Most southern Ikale towns had once been camps in the forest that later became small kingdoms.

The Ikale Kingdom had a strong cultural influence from Benin, which could be seen in their chieftaincy titles and monarchy system. This influence was due to Benin's commercial expansion. The most prominent Ikale towns were Ode-Aye, Ode-Erinje, Osooro, Ode-Irele, and Ikoya, the latter of which is thought to be the first of the Ikale cities.

The Ikale generally engaged in trade by bartering with the Ilaje for fish and other products in exchange for agricultural staple foods like yam, cassava, and oil.

## The Ondo Kingdom

The Ondo Kingdom was situated between Ikale and Ife. It was located in an area with thick forests and hills. Due to this, human settlement in this area was widely dispersed. And since the settlements were spaced away from each other, the people's dialect was markedly different in each settlement. Only three kingdoms were founded in this forest: Ondo, Idanre, and Epe.

We already know how Ondo was established, as its origin was discussed earlier in Chapter 1. The founders of Idanre were said to be Ife migrants who settled in the hilly area. Because they were mostly isolated from the other kingdoms, they did not fully imbibe the culture of the Ife migrants. Epe was originally a forest discovered by hunters from Ile-Ife. Epe is located close to Ijebu-Ode.

# Chapter 5 – The Economy of the Early Yoruba Kingdoms

The early Yoruba kingdoms were thriving in terms of the economy. The people participated in various activities such as farming, trading, craft specialization, hunting, fishing, and owning domestic animals. The early Yoruba kingdoms ran a patrilineage system; skills and crafts were passed down through the father's family line. As a result, lineages became known for a particular skill and/or craft set.

The development of the Yoruba economy can be divided into two eras, with the first one being the precolonial era, which spanned from the 11th century to the early 16th century. This era took place before European involvement in Yorubaland. The second era would be kickstarted with the arrival of European traders at the beginning of the 16th century, and it would last until the 19th century.

### The Precolonial Era (11th century to the early 16th century)

The creation of many cities, kingdoms, and towns in Yorubaland acted as a helpful catalyst in the transformation of its economic life in the 15th century. The Yoruba communities already had a form of a simple trade structure as early as the 11th century in the form of a barter system. As their civilization progressed, cowries were used as a form of payment. Soon, it became established as the main currency, and it was used for both commercial and social payments.

<u>The Second Era (The early 16<sup>th</sup> century to the 19<sup>th</sup> century)</u>

When the European coastal trade started in the early 16<sup>th</sup> century, it transformed many Yoruba kingdoms, ultimately shaping their economy. The transatlantic trade began with the slave trade. This aided the development of long-distance trade relations between the Europeans, Americans, and the early Yoruba people.

Later on, legitimate trade replaced the slave trade in the coastal regions. The kingdoms became a collection point for cocoa, palm oil, and kernels. These goods were brought to Lagos from inland kingdoms like Oyo and Benin, where it was then exported to Europe. During this period, trade with the Europeans was conducted only through Oyo, thus making it a monopolistic affair. Before any traders or merchants could conduct business with the Europeans, the Alaafin of Oyo had to issue a royal license.

# The Kingdoms and Their Economic Framework

As mentioned earlier, many activities contributed to the development of the Yoruba kingdoms' economic framework. The emergence of the royal cities, kingdoms, and other major towns widened opportunities in other occupations, such as house building, arts, entertainment, priestly occupations, health care and herbal occupations, and, perhaps most importantly, commerce. All of these later aided the development of the Yoruba civilization.

### Agriculture

The early Yoruba people carried out many economic activities, but the most predominant one was farming. Communities engaged in the production of crops mostly for feeding the local populace, but they also did so for commercial purposes. These goods were exchanged or sold for cowries in local and distant markets for materials they could not produce.

Agriculture had always been a pillar of the economy, even before most Yoruba kingdoms were created. While agriculture was not the only activity they engaged in, it constituted a large portion of their economy. One reason agriculture thrived in Yorubaland was the combination of suitable soils and adequate rains. This made most of the Yoruba homeland ideal for this activity. However, not all of the Yoruba lands were suitable for this purpose; there were places with lagoons, creeks, and swamps that were just not suitable for some crop types. These areas were the homes of the Ilaje, Itsekiri, Ijaw, and Ikale people.

The other belt, close to the north—the home of the Ekiti, Owo, Ondo, Ijebu, and Egba kingdoms—produced crops like yams, cassava, and cocoa. Yams also grew well in Ekiti and Akoko. One of the reasons for this was that these towns were located in partly forest and partly grassland areas. These greatly influenced the type of crop produced. For instance, the grasslands were best for cereal crops (mostly millet, maize, and guinea corn) and some beans. Therefore, foods and delicacies made from cereals and beans featured more prominently in the diets of those living there.

Oil palm was another crop that was often grown by the Yoruba people; however, these trees thrived more in regions with lightly forested areas. Palm oil and palm wine are the two most important byproducts of this tree, and they were used daily by most Yoruba people. However, other materials like oil palm fronds could be gotten from oil palm trees. Fronds are the main material used in making roofs, mats, and other craftwork.

Another crop grown for agricultural purposes was the kola nut, known as *Obi Abata* in Yoruba. Kola nuts grew in all parts of Yorubaland, but the first kingdom to produce it in large quantities for exportation was the Ife Kingdom. Later on, the exportation of kola nuts would spread to other parts of Yorubaland, like Ilesha, Owu,

Ijebu, and Egba. The farming and large-scale production of bitter kola, known in Yoruba as *orogbo*, also developed the same way. In areas like Ekiti, Oyo, and Ilesha, a particular bean tree grew, which yielded a bean called iru. This bean had a highly sought-after aromatic flavor. Indigo was also cultivated in commercial quantities and used to dye clothing.

The early Yoruba people also engaged in livestock farming. In some parts of Oyo, it was common for rich folks to own herds of cattle, goats, and sheep, which they reared and sold. This was done on a larger scale, so the owners required the help of laborers. The workers could have included both paid employees and slaves, and they could have come from within or beyond the kingdom. Most Yoruba people practiced the domestic rearing of livestock; however, this was done mainly by women. Some of the livestock included ducks, goats, sheep, pigeons, and chickens, most of which were reared in their homes, compounds, and/or neighborhoods. Some of the rich women had much livestock, which fetched them a considerable income.

## Commerce and Trade

The Yoruba trade practices put them ahead of other kingdoms, especially over landlocked towns and settlements. As early as the 16th century, there was already an established trade relationship between the Yoruba kingdoms and the Europeans. The region was well diversified in terms of agricultural products, which led to a specialization in production and manufacturing. Also, the Yorubas were blessed with some mineral resources. These specializations boosted the volume of internal trade, leading to increased productivity in the agricultural and industrial sectors. This increased productivity also led to a large number of products being exported beyond the Yoruba lands.

The Yoruba kingdoms became great places to trade, with their women ranking among the best traders in Africa. As productivity increased, long-distance trading surfaced, although the elites mostly carried it out during this period. Each Yoruba city had a king's marketplace, which was a way to generate, receive, distribute, and send out goods on a large scale. Cash crops and food crops like cocoa, kola nuts, and oil palms were all produced in mass quantities. This was aided by the region's topography, good weather, and high-quality soil.

The Yoruba trading empire covered many kingdoms and extended as far as the Senegal River in the west and the Congo to the east. Even within the Yoruba empire itself, many trading communities and routes were established. Two good examples are the Hausa and Nupe trading communities. Also, traders from the far north, like the Sahara, became a daily part of the trading communities. The Yoruba held the Nupe and Hausa traders in high regard, and they went out of their way to allocate space inside or close to the palace or marketplace for these traders.

As time went on, there was an increase in the number of Hausa and Nupe traders frequenting the Yoruba markets. Since many of the Hausa traders were Muslim, the kings gave them land to erect their own mosque, which was usually close to the marketplace. This made it easy for them to observe their prayer break, as they would be close to their stores or market stalls. Other communities in eastern and southern Yorubaland provided residences for these foreign traders. Through trade, the northerners were able to spread the Muslim religion to the Yorubas.

As you can see, many Yoruba kingdoms' economies and trade were something to behold back then. It certainly seems that they could hold their own among the best.

Manufacturing and Production

The exponential growth of the Yoruba economy gave rise to the manufacturing and production sector. This played a huge role in the development of many communities within Yorubaland.

The agricultural boom and subsequent storage problems led to many products being converted into something new. Crops like maize, cassava, and millet were used to manufacture new food delicacies. Maize was converted to pap, which could be in a semi-liquid form (*ogi*) or a solid form (*eko* or *agidi*). This delicacy was mostly manufactured in the Osun and Oyo region, from where it was exported to neighboring kingdoms and regions.

Processing cassava tubers into other products was also a productive and lucrative business for all the Yoruba kingdoms. The cassava tuber is still one of the most valuable plant products in West Africa. About 250,000 tons of garri (the creamy flour made from cassava) are prepared in Nigeria yearly. Cassava originated from South America, and it was made known to Nigerians in the 16th century by European colonizers from Portugal while trading for slaves. Its value was not truly known until freed slaves started returning in the early 19th century and introduced new processing methods for the crop. Cassava is a very versatile product that can be processed into different things, including fufu (a sticky dough), garri, animal feed, starches for gluing papers, and textiles.

Garri is the most common byproduct of cassava, and it is made by slicing and grating the tubers, then soaking and fermenting them for a few days before grinding and finally frying the cassava flakes. Garri has many health benefits because it contains phosphorus, calcium, and riboflavin. The starch in cassava is called resistant starch, which is good for industrial sizing and gluing purposes. The Yoruba kingdoms made a lot of income from cassava byproducts by exporting them to other regions. This had a positive impact on the Yoruba kingdoms' commerce at the time.

Another craft that boosted their commercial activities was cloth dyeing. This craft was usually passed from mother to daughter for many generations. Towns close to the Osun Valley were known for their beautiful and excellent dye work. Dyed clothes became an important fashion trend during the Second Era, with the demand for this product increasing across the regions as time passed. Some of the techniques employed in this production process include tie-dye. This involves tying the cloth into different shapes before dipping it into the dye. The demand for this product significantly boosted the trade of the Osun region.

In the early years of the Yoruba kingdoms, the production of jasper and carnelian beads came into the spotlight, especially in the Oyo and Ife kingdoms. These beads were worn mainly by royals, chiefs, and prominent figures in society. They were worn on the wrists, necks, and ankles, and they signified honor, power, authority, and prestige for the wearer. It was also believed that the beads would bring them good fortune. The production of these beads was a laborious process, and it required skill, strength, and considerable patience. Findings indicate that it could take professionals about four to seven days, with ten hours of dedicated work each day, for one bead worker to produce a necklace containing eighteen to twenty beads.

Beads represented one's power, so if someone increased their station, they would wear different beads to show this. Jasper was the preferred gemstone to signify power. Later on, some other gems, like carnelian and the red and brown chalcedonic quartzes, would come into play. Several varieties of these beads have been found in Oyo, Ile-Ife, Ilesha, and Benin. Due to the importance attached to these beads, they become desirable and valuable, making the production of beads a lucrative and attractive one, thus increasing the economic revenue of the kingdom at large.

*Involvement of the Europeans and the Slave Trade*

The trade relationship between the European and African nations developed in the economic era of the African continent. For West Africa, especially in the Gulf of Benin and along its coasts, the European merchants had a well-established trading population regulated by intelligent and experienced African rulers. Some goods imported to West Africa in large volumes included cloth, iron, raw copper, and cowry shells, the latter of which was used as a medium of exchange by the local populations along the West African coast. Other luxury items, such as jewelry, alcohol, and mirrors, were also imported.

The Portuguese were the first to arrive in West Africa when they were sailing around the Atlantic to seek a path into Africa that reached Asia. They arrived on the coast of Benin in the late 15th century. At that time, the Kingdom of Benin and most of the Yoruba kingdoms had already become quite advanced; for instance, kingdoms like Ife, Ondo, Oyo, and some Ekiti kingdoms were already trading on a large scale.

The Portuguese set up a factory (a trading post) at the Benin port town of Ughoton and in other places like Ode-Itsekiri. Later on, more trading posts were established by the Europeans along the Gulf of Benin. The Portuguese traders were also charmed by the island of Eko, which they would later rename Lagos. However, access to the island was very difficult due to the sand bars and dunes surrounding it.

This wasn't the only problem the Europeans faced. Even with the availability of factories in Yorubaland, none could serve as a natural harbor for large ships. And even if there was, the Ijebu and Ilaje coasts weren't as accessible as Lagos. Thus, the major European trade centers with the Yoruba interior kingdoms weren't located on the Yoruba coastline but rather in the Kingdom of Benin. Nevertheless, there were still some trading posts on the Yoruba coast, mainly on Lagos and the Ijebu coast; these grew gradually during the 16th century.

Later on, in the early 18th century, the European started a new port in Badagry, which is close to Lagos. However, when compared to Ughoton, it was relatively smaller. Still, it would still serve its purpose, as goods could easily reach the interior parts of the Yoruba kingdoms from Badagry.

When Badagry first started, it was mostly used for slave trading, which brought the Atlantic market closer to the Egba and Ijebu coasts in southern Yorubaland. The transatlantic slave trade commenced during the 15ᵗʰ century when Portugal and other European kingdoms first landed on the shores of West Africa. The Portuguese started kidnapping some of the natives of these regions, who were then taken back to Europe and sold into slavery.

Consequently, this resulted in the early development of Ijebu because it had access to the Europeans and their imports, which eventually opened up Osun and other frontiers to the Atlantic slave trade. The Ijebu traders were the top transporters of European imports, obtaining mostly cowries, tobacco, and textiles, in particular damask and silk materials.

The practice of slavery had long been established in Europe, as Europeans had enslaved each other for thousands of years. And this practice also already existed in Yorubaland long before the Europeans landed on the West African coast. However, the practice of buying and selling slaves was extremely rare. As of then, slaves, known as an *eru*, were only gotten as spoils of war. Often, the slaves would end up as palace servants or maids. Sometimes, the king might reward slaves to the worthiest of his cabinet and some of those who made the conquest possible. Thus, the Yoruba people owned slaves, but buying or selling them was not in vogue before the Europeans arrived.

Also, if an *eru* was allocated to the palace, he could have risen in rank depending solely on his character, loyalty, and strength. In Yorubaland, an *eru* may have become influential enough to the extent of marrying a princess. The men who didn't serve inside the palace may have been allowed to raise crops of their own on his master's farmland or establish some other enterprise; of course, he needed permission to do so. Unless he had some serious character blemish, he would usually inherit some of his master's belongings.

At the peak of the transatlantic slave trade, these *erus*, which were obtained through war, were sold as slaves. In the precolonial era, there were many Yoruba traders, but few eventually became wholesalers, who were referred to as an *alajapa*. These *alajapas* had rankings, and their leaders formed an association called the Parayoki, meaning "merchant's guild." Slave trading was an expensive endeavor, as it involved paying for the welfare and transportation of the slaves, traders, and soldiers. The soldiers were necessary to control the slaves and also to launch warfare on villages to capture more slaves.

War chiefs and politicians usually had soldiers working for them. Some of these soldiers were free and chose to work for their bosses; however, the majority of them were usually *erus* captured during previous wars. These soldiers were then sent to battle neighboring villages or communities that were known to be weak. After the battle, the war chief would lay claim to 40 to 60 percent of the slaves captured by the free soldiers and 60 to 80 percent of the slaves captured by the *eru* soldiers. The war chief could then sell these slaves with the help of traders and *alajapas*. The soldiers themselves also made money by selling the slaves to the Parayoki.

The traders would then transport these purchased slaves to the markets and ports to be purchased by the Europeans. The traders ensured their safe transport by employing soldiers. The Europeans, in turn, ensured the capture of slaves by providing weapons to the traders, who proceeded to sell those weapons to the soldiers. This way, all parties worked together to guarantee the flow of slaves. And on top of this, the Europeans and the traders also forged relationships and made alliances. Examples of some of the alliances include marriage arrangements, child fostering, and written contracts. These all continued until around the 1860s.

# Institutions and Features That Aided the Yorubaland's Economy

While the Yoruba economy was a booming one, special institutions boosted it and made everything well organized.

### Royal Finances

As with most monarchies, the royal finances were taken from tolls and taxes on commerce. All merchandise was taxed, except those obtained from peasants or local farmers. The king appointed an *onibode*, meaning "gatekeeper," to guard the kingdom and collect these taxes. His office was an important one, and it often became a hereditary position in most kingdoms.

The amount of revenue generated from tolls depended on the volume of trade passing through the kingdom's gates. The more accessible and safer a route was, the more people would travel it. Due to this, each kingdom took great care in maintaining its major trades routes and ensuring they were safe, which, in turn, influenced the amount of trade that entered the kingdom.

Another source of income for the monarchy was the taxes and tolls taken from the king's marketplace. The king's servant had a right to collect customary payments on each *iso* (trader's stall) on his behalf. The king could also collect taxes on special goods or demand payment or gifts on days of special occasions, like festivals. The king's wives could also receive gifts from traders whenever they visited the market, same with the palace servants.

The king also generated revenue by imposing taxes and levies on conquered towns and villages. These conquered towns and villages, known as *ereko*, would send tribute, gifts, and slaves to the kingdom now overseeing them. Although this practice varied from kingdom to kingdom, Oyo-Ile was the most known for using this practice. At the height of Oyo's glory, all of its *ereko* would send annual gifts and taxes, which were then used for the kingdom's development.

There were also traditions, rules, and customs that allowed the king to generate revenue. For instance, when the king settled a dispute between houses or lineages, both sides were required to send gifts to the king in appreciation. Also, some animals like leopards and elephants were regarded as royal property, so any hunter who succeeded in killing these animals must surrender them to the king. During a marriage or the funeral of a notable figure, part of the rites included sending gifts to the king. These gifts amounted to a substantial income for the ruler, thus making him richer than even the richest citizen.

The king also generated revenue from agriculture. In most kingdoms, kings had a large plot of land known as *oko oba*, meaning the "king's farmland," where his slaves and servants farmed produce for him daily. This farm was out of bounds from the general population, and produce from the farm was used to feed the king and his large household. Some of this produce was also taken to the market to sell. Other traders could only sell their produce of the same type once the king's produce had been sold.

### Savings and Capital Formation

The emergence of more civilized kingdoms brought about a significant transformation in the manufacturing, commerce, and agricultural sectors. This induced changes in some economic activities like saving, although some forms of this practice already existed. The development of urban settlements brought about money-saving practices like the *ajo*, *esusu*, and other money-lending institutions.

The growth of the agricultural, commercial, and manufacturing sectors ensured an increase in the people's income. Also, major expenditures and family occasions like weddings and funerals led to the establishment of a savings system and other financial institutions. *Ajo*, meaning "gathering together," started with the development of urban Yoruba settlements. *Ajo* involved giving a contribution to a trustworthy person among a social group, whether it be an age group, traders' association, or agbo-ile. Each individual participating in *ajo* contributed the same amount of money at regular intervals to avoid confusion. Before an individual could collect his accumulated savings, he first needed to give the *alajo* (the one in charge of the savings) an advance notice.

There was one big problem with the *ajo* system: a low level of security. Often, the *alajo* was also a moneylender, which meant that he could loan out the money that had been deposited with him. If any loan went bad, his obligations to those saving with him would be disrupted. Usually, the people didn't get their money back, as the *alajo* would run away.

Another savings system that was practiced was the *esusu*, meaning "pooling and disbursing." With the *esusu*, each group member agreed upon a fixed sum to be paid at a specified time. The total amount of the money was paid to an individual in the group in rotation; thus, members of the group took turns collecting the total amount of money.

The *esusu* was well established in all parts of Yorubaland, with many *esusu* groups existing at once. The *esusu* had a president who oversaw the contributions and disbursement of money. The order in which the *esusu* would be disbursed was agreed upon before any contributions took place. Also, penalties and laws were stated before they started contributing. The lateness of any member in contributing was considered a serious offense. Any member expelled from the group had to wait until the end of the cycle when everyone had taken their share.

The *esusu* greatly aided low-income individuals in the early Yoruba kingdoms, and it still does. The *esusu* and *ajo* systems operated more like the banks we see today, and they are still impacting Yoruba communities to this day.

### Loans and the Credit System

While the *ajo* and *esusu* systems offered loans, they were not available to the general public. This prompted the development of other types of loans and credit that were available to anyone. The first people to start handing out loans to the public were wealthy traders; however, others went fully into the trade and became moneylenders.

These moneylenders were known as *olowo-ele*, and they were providers of interest-bearing loans. These moneylenders did not necessarily have to accept payments of interest in cash; sometimes, they took payments in the form of goods, labor, or services. Another form of loans was the *iwofa*, but in this case, a person was given to serve the lender. Until the money was paid in full, the person had to serve the lender.

Another type of loan involved a farmer surrendering his farm. The lenders would then harvest it as a loan repayment. If anyone defaulted on the loan, the creditor could report the culprit to his lineage head. If that didn't work, the moneylender might employ the help of a distrainer. He would impose his presence on the debtor anytime and anyplace, giving the debtor no privacy. The distrainer was untouchable, as harming him meant violating the authority of the person who had employed him. Using a distrainer proved to be an effective method of recovering loans, as he attacked not only the debtor but also his lineage.

Oftentimes, to avoid the embarrassment and stigma that came from borrowing and defaulting on a loan, a compound usually came together to contribute the money or offer a satisfactory payment to the creditor.

### The Impact of Women on the Economy

The Yorubas regarded some occupations as solely belonging to the male domain. For instance, women were exempted from tougher farm work. The women were assigned menial jobs and were more of a backup for the men. They cooked, fetched water, carried firewood, and did light harvesting. Although they were not heavily involved in the farm work, they were responsible for selling agricultural produce. Women were also heavily involved in crafts and the manufacturing processes; however, processes like metal smelting were still reserved for men. The Yoruba women were dominant in the kingdoms' commercial life. They created the trade network that shaped the Yoruba economy.

# Chapter 6 – The Politics of the Early Yoruba Kingdoms

New cities and settlements were mostly created in two different ways. The first was through wars. Conflicts caused the destruction of pre-existing settlements and resulted in the victor merging their population with the original settlers, as seen with the founders of Ilesha and Owo. The other way was building upon existing infrastructure, like what Obanta and his people did in Ijebu-Ode, where they created structures typical of a Yoruba city, like the king's palace, king's marketplace, and the city walls. Awamaro did the same when founding Ado in Ekiti; he left the original settlers at the foot of the Olota Rock and continued building the city around the rock.

The populations in most Yoruba cities or towns were segmented; each segment or quarter had its own leaders, known as chiefs. This was especially true for the early settlers. The system of government in most Yoruba cities was a monarchial one since most of these kingdoms had their roots from Ile-Ife. Most of the migrants who left Ife to settle in a new place recreated the culture and traditions of their home kingdom wherever they settled.

The king's council was formed of chiefs from all the quarters of the city. The chief of the largest quarter was most likely the leader of the council, although leadership might have been based on other factors, such as ancestry, history, chivalry, and how famous or close they were to the king. Whenever a new group joined the city, the king's council met to decide the appropriate position for the new group leader. As the city grew, the king's council made recommendations to the king to create lower chieftaincy titles for the streets of each quarter, which would help the quarter chiefs.

The king's council, which usually only consisted of five or seven men, met with the king daily to make decisions concerning the kingdom; these decisions were then presented to the people as the king's decision. The council served as the highest court in the land, and it could only be overturned by the king. By law, the king could not make decisions without approval from the council. The council had different names, but it functioned roughly in the same manner in the different kingdoms. Other lower-level chiefs also met with the king, as his decisions were communicated to the chiefs for deliberation. If need be, they sent a message back to the king for modifications. When the king's decision was finalized, it was communicated through a town crier, who would go into the streets late in the evening and use a gong to garner attention before relaying the king's message. The chiefs would then see to it that the king's orders were carried out properly in their quarters.

The responsibility of selecting a new king fell mainly on the king's council. The throne was hereditary, but it was not always passed directly from father to son. All male members of the royal family, including sons and grandsons of former kings, were qualified to be king. Primogeniture was rejected in Yoruba culture to reduce the incidence of parricide among the crown princes. The crown prince, known as the Aremo, basically reigned alongside his father and performed royal duties. In the event of his father's death, the Aremo was expected to commit suicide. In 1858, Alaafin Atiba abolished the law, and he was succeeded by his son, Adelu, after his passing.

However, the Aremo still had to be elected by the council to become king. If he was found unworthy of such a position, he had to leave the city and live in a private residence in a satellite town of the kingdom. Though this course of action was not obligatory, it was usually inevitable since the new king's authority would supersede his own. He could also choose to die with his father.

The council's decision on who was to be king was final, and they viewed any agitation from competitors as a crime. Though the council members could be lobbied, they held themselves to a very high moral standard. After all, a high level of accountability and discipline was expected of them. No member of the council was allowed to take gifts from those seeking the title or even from members of the public.

Once a decision had been reached by the kingmakers, the person who was chosen was handed over to the right officials and priests for the coronation process to begin. The new king would live outside the palace in a compound for a few months, where he was instructed on how to behave and what to do and not to do before completing the necessary rituals. The kingmaker's council could also remove a king if they gauged his actions to be beyond the established controls of royal power; in other words, if he was immoral, greedy, or had tyrannical tendencies.

There were different methods of removing such a king from the throne. The council might give him an empty calabash (a type of gourd). Once the king opened it, he knew the council wanted him to commit suicide. He could also be given a dish of parrot eggs, which would have the same message as an empty calabash. The king also might be urged "to go to sleep" if it seemed he could not bear the burden of kingship. These methods of removal were performed to dignify the position of the king.

# Prominent Wars and Treaties

The warlike nature of the Yoruba people is well known, so it is not surprising they were involved in many wars. With the slave trade thriving in the region, warlike individuals dominated. Still, many of the wars were fought at the behest of kings.

Gaha, an elite in the Oyo Empire during the 18th century, was named Bashorun (similar to a prime minister) in 1754. This event marked a turn for the worse in the history of the Oyo Empire. Gaha coveted the power and authorities of the Alaafin and deposed almost all the Alaafins he served under. Bashorun Gaha served five Alaafins; he influenced the death of four of them and tried to depose the fifth one (Alaafin Abiodun). However, he was unsuccessful in his last endeavor. This led to his death and the massacre of his family. Gaha was a great military leader and was beloved by his people for winning wars and protecting them from the tyranny of the Alaafins, but his own tyranny led to his downfall. His actions also kick-started the fall of the Oyo Empire.

After the death of Alaafin Abiodun of Oyo (r. c. 1770-1789), his son or cousin known as Awole (also spelled as Aole) was chosen as the new king. However, his reign was short and unhappy, which further contributed to the decline of the Oyo Empire.

According to custom, after Awole's coronation, the king sent out an expedition party to fight and destroy his enemies. During Awole's reign, which lasted from 1789 to 1796, he told the expedition party to eliminate the Baale (head of the clan) of Apomu, a town located in modern-day Ondo State.

This battle took place during a time when the slave trade was popular. Before Alaafin Abiodun had passed, he had agreed with both the Olowu of Owu and the Ooni of Ife to prevent the kidnapping and selling of their people; they, in turn, asked the Baale of Apomu to help prevent such events from happening again.

Awole traded along those routes with a friend. On one occasion, he decided to sell his friend, and it was reported to the Baale of Apomu that an Oyo man was being sold as a slave. The Baale of Apomu swooped in to arrest the individuals involved in this act of slavery. In the course of the investigation, it was discovered that Awole was the culprit. But since Awole was a prince, he could not be dealt with to the full extent of the law. The Baale didn't want judgment to be miscarried, so Awole was ordered to be flogged. Ever since then, Awole held a grudge, and this grudge manifested into actual conflict once he became king.

The Baale of Apomu ran to the Ooni of Ife to seek aid, but the Ooni could not save him. The Baale of Apomu committed suicide to appease the offended Alaafin and to prevent him from destroying his people. Regardless, according to tradition, an expedition had to be sent out, and Awole was asked who his enemies were. He replied, saying, "My enemies are too formidable." When further pressed to reveal his enemy, he named Afonja, a powerful chief. It is likely Awole named him because the Alaafin could see him being a potential source of trouble.

During this period, Afonja resided in Ilorin, an important military outpost in Oyo. Afonja held the title of Kakanfo, which is similar to a modern-day general. However, it took some maneuvering to get the title. After the former Kakanfo's death, Afonja demanded the title. But since he was a prince connected to the throne through his mother's side, the title was deemed to be beneath him. Eventually, the king granted Afonja's wish, as Afonja was a powerful individual who was willing to go to war for the title. Also, taking any action against Afonja would mean the outbreak of a civil war because many chiefs were loyal to him. Nevertheless, Afonja was added to Awole's list of enemies.

Eventually, though, other chiefs turned against Awole, namely Asamu the Bashorun. His quarrel with the Bashorun was over a Hausa trader who had lost his goods. This trader directly implored the king to help him get back his Koran, which was incredibly important to him. The king ordered the goods to be found and returned, but the Koran was not returned, although the trader did receive all of his other goods. The Hausa man pled for his priceless possession, and the king insisted the search must continue. The Bashorun, who knew where it was, refused to tell the king the truth. The king was deeply insulted by this, and he apparently said, "Has it come to this, that my commands cannot be obeyed in my capital? Must it be said that I failed to redress the grievance of a stranger in my town? That he appealed to me in vain?"

So, the king said to the Bashorun, "If you cannot find it, my father [the deity Shango, who was known for punishing thieves by burning the perpetrator's house] will find it for me." The next day, lightning struck the Bashorun's house, and the Bashorun was angry with the king for making him out to be a liar and a thief.

Another chief who was added to Awole's long list of enemies was Lafianu the Owota (believed to be a title of some kind). Lafianu had once protected Jankalawa, a man who had offended the late king and escaped to Bariba country (located in modern-day northeast Benin). After Alaafin Abiodun's death, Jankalawa returned, which annoyed the late king's wives. They complained and implored Awole to avenge this slight against the prior king.

After numerous appeals, Awole yielded and ordered the arrest and execution of Jankalawa. The Owota was angry for not being consulted, as the man had been under his protection. His ego was bruised since he had not been respected. So, the Bashorun, Kakanfo, and Owota became the king's enemies, and they conspired together.

The king was unwilling to confront the Kakanfo head-on, but he was advised by his counselors to send the Kakanfo to attack Iwere, a fortified city. Weapons were practically useless against the Iwere army. Back then, the Kakanfo's oath of office stated that he must either win within three months or die. Since Iwere was impregnable, he would more than likely have to commit suicide. The counselors decided not to warn the Kakanfo about this until he had been led to the foot of the hill where Iwere was built.

However, intelligence about the conspiracy reached the Kakanfo. Upon reaching the foot of the Iwere hill, Kakanfo attacked the royal party, which consisted of the king's brother, eunuchs, soldiers, and slaves, claiming that the king had set him and his army up for defeat by fighting an impregnable town.

Turning the army around, the Kakanfo, with the Bashorun and Owota at the head of the army, turned toward Oyo. The king sent word to inquire if the expedition was successful. The conspiring chiefs then sent word back, saying the royal party had insulted them and that the events that had unfolded had been unfortunate. The king asked them to come and personally inform him. However, the rebelling chiefs camped outside the capital and sent the king an empty calabash, a message telling him to commit suicide.

But before committing suicide, Awole took three arrows and an earthenware dish. He fired the arrows to the north, south, and west, uttering a curse upon the chiefs. Since they had been disloyal and disobedient to him, their children would be disobedient; when sent out on an errand, they would never return. Awole then broke the dish, which signified that the curse could not be reversed. After doing this, Awole took some poison and died. After pillaging the city and the palace, the chiefs and their forces disbanded. This ended an unhappy seven-year reign and began the nation's disintegration into tribal wars for independence.

The successor, Prince Adebo, became king at an unfortunate time, and he only spent 130 days on the throne. During this period, rebellion was the order of the day; he was essentially a king with no authority and power. Tributes were not sent to him, law and justice were subverted, and towns attacked each other to increase their wealth and power. Even the king's messengers no longer respected the ruler. Afonja the Kakanfo and Opele, the Baale of Gbogun, were the first to declare independence. Opele was the only chief Afonja respected, but he, unfortunately, died while fighting. Having no real rival, Afonja decided to pillage the towns and cities surrounding the capital to isolate it. In around 1817, to further strengthen his position, Afonja invited a Muslim priest named Alimi to Ilorin to serve as his personal priest. Alimi accepted the position and also brought some Hausa slaves, whom Afonja deployed as soldiers. Afonja also invited a rich friend named Solagberu, who could potentially help finance the war effort.

Ojo Agunbambaru was one of Bashorun Gaha's children who had survived the massacre; he escaped to Bariba country. After becoming aware of the happenings in the state, he decided to come back and exploit the opportunity to avenge his father and get a title for himself. He brought a large army from Bariba and killed chiefs who were friends or allies with Afonja, doing so under the pretext of avenging the king.

In total, it is thought that Ojo killed more than one hundred chiefs who could oppose him, with Lafianu the Owota being his first victim. After taking over Oyo, Ojo set a course for Ilorin to fight Afonja. Ojo's campaign did not enjoy the support of other chiefs due to the indiscriminate killings of rulers. If Ojo had not killed so many chiefs, it is possible that they might have pitied his plight and joined him in going to war against Afonja, as he was only growing stronger as time passed.

Ojo also threatened Adegun, the Onikoyi of Ikoyi-Ile, who could have been a great addition to his camp. Ikoyi-Ile was located ten miles from Oyo, and it was founded by a different Adegun, one of Oduduwa's descendants.

Ojo's army wreaked so much destruction that towns deserted as it approached. The Oyo people following him did so out of fear, not out of loyalty. The Onikoyi, Afonja's friend, even secretly joined Ojo's ranks, keeping Afonja abreast of Ojo's policies and movements. The Oyo people and the Onikoyi hatched a plan to desert Ojo during the heat of battle.

Afonja met Ojo's army far from Ilorin, and a battle ensued. Afonja was defeated in three engagements, costing him most of his soldiers. Afonja fled back to Ilorin to fortify the city's defenses with stockades made from shea and locust trees since Ilorin had no walls.

The Onikoyi and his men besieged Ilorin, and Afonja had a hard time beating the attackers back. The Onikoyi sent a message to Afonja to persevere a bit longer. Right when the city was about to fall, the Onikoyi and his men retreated, leaving Ojo behind, who lost the battle. Ojo was deserted by those he thought he was fighting for. Somehow, he managed to escape death, and he retreated back to Bariba country.

# The Battle of Ogele (1824–1825)

In 1823/24, Afonja was killed by the Hausa Jamas (enlisted soldiers). They had been ordered to do so by Alimi, Afonja's priest. This shocked and bewildered everyone since Afonja had been the Kakanfo. It also threw the Yoruba nation into disarray. A conclave was called to unite and avenge his death, not knowing that Alimi, who was now controlling Ilorin, had prepared for the conflict. (This was how Islam took hold in Ilorin, as many Yoruba Muslim clerics started to emerge. From here on, the religion began to spread through the clerics until it became popular among the commoners and the people in the Yoruba palaces.)

Alimi had studied the Yorubas for a long time and understood how to defeat them. Toyeje, the Baale of Ogbomoso (a town close to Oyo-Ile), was elevated to the position of Kakanfo, and he united the whole nation to chase the Fulanis out of Ilorin. (The Fulanis remain one of the largest ethnic groups in West Africa, and they are primarily Muslim.) Toyeje and his men decided to camp in Ogele, located in the Edo region. There, they fought the Fulanis, who were led by Solagberu, Afonja's rich friend.

The Fulanis were victorious in this bloody battle, which led to the destruction of many towns. The Fulanis pursued the Yorubas vigorously, so the refugees only had a limited amount of time to choose a few of their personal things to take or else risk being captured. Children went missing, and older people were sometimes left behind. The people were bereft of money and items of value, reducing them to a life of poverty and misery. Thus, the Yorubas' first attempt to retrieve Ilorin resulted in a sound defeat for them.

# The Mugbamugba War (1824–1825)

After a brief period of rest, the Yorubas decided to rally together again. This time, they were determined to chase the Fulanis and the Hausa Jamas out of Ilorin. The Yorubas allied with the king of Rabbah (believed to be the Nupe king, possibly Majiya II). The war commenced sometime between March and April.

Many towns and villages were already devasted from the previous war, so by the time the second war erupted, the country was on the brink of famine. Since farmlands were not tended to because of the previous war, the Yorubas and the Fulanis devoured the food they found on Ilorin farms, and when nothing was left, they started eating locust fruit (*igba*)—hence the name "Mugbamugba." (*Mu* in Yoruba means to take, drink, or bring something. Thus, *mu igba* (put together as "mugba") would mean to take locust fruit.)

The Fulanis and their calvary triumphed against the Yorubas because they did not understand how to defeat the Fulani horsemen, causing them to lose courage and strength. During the battle, the Fulanis employed a new tactic in which they left their main cavalry at the rear of the Yorubas and attacked with a few horsemen during the heat of battle. This allowed the cavalry to quickly attack from the rear and destroy the Yorubas.

The Fulanis triumphed easily with their horses in open fields, and when the Yorubas fled to fortified towns, they only found famine, which was further exacerbated by the ensuing siege. The king escaped to Rabbah, leaving the Yorubas at the mercy of the Fulanis, who were now emboldened with the taste of victory. They decided to pillage all of the towns in the direction of Ofa, Erin, and Igbona, with their inhabitants and kings escaping to Ikoyi.

# The Battle of Pamo (1825–1831)

Ilorin was eventually delivered into the hands of the Fulanis. After the death of Alimi (the sources are unclear of when this actually happened, which is a problem that plagues much of Yoruba history), he was succeeded by Abdulsalami, his son, who became the first Emir of Ilorin, solidifying the family's claim to Ilorin. To better understand the family's desire to claim Ilorin, we have to go back and look at Alimi's history in the city. During Afonja's reign, Alimi had been greatly displeased with Afonja's excesses and wanted to leave. He had never intended to stay for long in the first place, but he was begged to stay in the city by the Yoruba leaders. They wanted someone to keep Afonja's ambitions in check, and they greatly respected the Muslim priest.

So, he sent for his wife, who was apparently barren. His wife consulted with another Muslim priest about her barrenness, and she was told to give a slave as alms to a distinguished Muslim priest. The greatest priest she knew was her own husband, so she gave one of her female slaves to Alimi. This slave gave birth to Alimi's two eldest sons: Abdulsalami and Shitta. Alimi's wife also became pregnant, and she gave birth to another son whom they named Sumonu (also known as Beribepo). Alimi married again, and this wife gave birth to yet another son. Together, these four sons would inherit Alimi's properties after his death.

Abdulsalami and his full-blooded brother took over the city, leaving nothing to the first wife's son. It is unknown if the fourth son received anything; it is possible that he had died by this time. With the brothers' newfound power, they decided to conquer Yorubaland. They played unsuspecting Yoruba leaders against each other. These leaders were jealous of each other's strength, fame, and military conquests, and their antagonistic and petty feelings led to many defeats among the Yoruba chiefs, who stood no chance without being united.

So, Kakanfo Toyeje quarreled with Onikoyi Adegun, which led to war. To strengthen his position, the Kakanfo formed a league with the Timi of Ede, Solagberu of Ilorin, and the Oluiwo of Iwo to besiege Ikoyi. Solagberu already had a personal vendetta against Adegun for not paying him the proper homage.

The allied forces camped in the city of Pamo, and from there, they fought against the people of Ikoyi, almost subduing the city. A refugee living in the city actually saved the day by asking the Onikoyi if he could be allowed to use his wisdom to save the city. The Onikoyi was tired of the war and looking for a peaceful settlement, so this request was granted. The refugee decided to send a private messenger to Abdulsalami in the Onikoyi's name, saying he pledged allegiance to the Emir of Ilorin. Upon hearing this, the Emir told Solagberu to withdraw, but he refused.

After successive orders with the same outcome, Abdulsalami asked the chiefs, princes, and any loyal personnel to immediately return home, leaving Solagberu alone. In order to raise the siege, the Emir sent out another force to reinforce Ikoyi. But after reaching Ikoyi, the Ilorin soldiers drank themselves to a stupor for ten days. On the eleventh day, they joined forces with the Onikoyi. They defeated Kakanfo Toyeje's army, leaving great men dead on the battlefield.

Solagberu fled back to Ilorin. Although he was allowed to stay there, Solagberu greatly resented the Emir, a feeling that was reciprocated. Every incident in the city seemed to increase the tensions between the two men until it led to war. The Emir besieged Okesuna, where Solagberu was residing. Eventually, the people at Okesuna had to face facts, as they were all suffering from famine. In the end, Solagberu was killed.

Abdulsalami was now without a major opponent. The Onikoyi had pledged allegiance to him, and the Kakanfo's army was destroyed. Thus, Abdulsalami decided to declare himself the king of Yorubaland. The rest of the Yoruba towns were made to give tribute. Abdulsalami used his Jamas to help with this, and they ended up oppressing the people, taking their livestock, wives, and children whenever they chose to.

# The Owu War

With the Fulanis victorious and most of the kingdoms in disarray, each state claimed independence and sovereignty and fought for its own interest. The people of Ijebu and Ife toward the south and east, respectively, allied together against the Owus.

The Owu people were known for their stubbornness, immorality, hardiness, and arrogance. Although the Owus' mannerisms were different from the Oyos, they always stood by the Alaafin. The Owu people were also great warriors, with their weapons of choice being the cutlass and the bow and arrow.

The war between the Owus and Oyos started during the reign of King Abiodun, who gave an order saying that the Oyo people must not be kidnapped and sold at Apomu. In around 1821, a similar order came from Onikoyi Adegun and Kakanfo Toyeje. When their armies carried out these orders, they ended up destroying several towns, all of which were Ife territories.

The Ooni of Ife was greatly displeased by this, and he declared war on Owu, entrusting the command to Singunsin. The party camped at the confluence of the Osun and Oba Rivers in a farm village called Dariagbon.

The Ife considered themselves to be very brave and warlike, so they thought victory would be easy. However, the Owus, upon hearing the news of the war, immediately set out to engage their enemies, whom they annihilated. The few Ifes who lived to tell the tale escaped to Iwo, but fearing reprisal from the Owus, the king of Iwo told the Ifes they could not stay. However, he sympathized so much with their cause that he allowed them to gather their forces together and prepare for another attack in Adunbieiye, which was nearby. The Ifes remained there for around five years due to both shame and the lack of reinforcements.

In the meantime, the Owus arrogant nature caused another incident; they destroyed Apomu over a trading dispute with Ijebu. This resulted in the death of many Ijebus.

The king of Iwo advised the Ifes and Ijebus to ally against the Owus. The Ifes reinforced their forgotten army in Adunbieiye, and the Ijebus, being closer to the coast, had access to guns from the Europeans and were well-armed. The Owus heard about the war and rushed out with cutlass in hand to meet the Ijebus. However, their weapons were no match for the Ijebus' guns, and the Owus incurred heavy losses.

After regrouping, the Owus engaged the Ijebus again, suffering yet another loss. The Owus retreated a short distance away, where they regrouped and engaged the Ijebus once more. They were again defeated. With their courage broken and resigned to their fate, they retreated to Owu to fortify their city for the siege they knew was coming.

The Ijebus and Ifes encamped under a tree known as the Ogungun. They engaged the Owus, who defended their town against the siege for years (some historians say five years, while others say seven). But even though the people fought bravely, famine could not be avoided. The Owus ate large beans called *popondo* or *awuje*, which were thought to be unfit to eat as food.

The allied forces could neither crush the wall nor destroy the gate. Eventually, the Olowu opened a gate and escaped to Erunmu, one of the towns under Owu rule. The chief of Erunmu, though related to the Ooni of Ife, protected the Olowu. After the fall of Owu, the chief of Erunmu was pardoned for assisting the Owu ruler.

After the conquest of Owu, the allies returned to their camp by the Ogungun tree. There, they agreed that Owu should never be rebuilt. Oje, the closest town to Owu, could not expand beyond the Ogungun tree. The Owu land was still cultivated, but no building was placed on its soil. In 1873, someone built a farmhouse on Owu land. The home was immediately ordered to be destroyed, and the man was fined for putting it up. So, Owu remains unbuilt, with its ancient structures abandoned. However, people are living around the ruins, and many Owu descendants moved to Abeokuta, which is located in present-day Ogun State, Nigeria.

This war on Owu contains a historical first, as it was the first time gunpowder weapons were used by the Yorubas to fight. The war also laid the foundation for the destruction of other Egba towns and the creation of modern-day Abeokuta and Ibadan, the latter of which is located in present-day Oyo State, Nigeria. Ibadan is also the largest capital city in Nigeria in terms of geographical area.

# Chapter 7 – The Rise and Fall of the Oyo Empire

The history of Yorubaland is not complete without mentioning the great Oyo Empire. The early Oyo Empire consisted of parts of what is currently western Nigeria and the eastern Republic of Benin. The ancient Oyo Empire was founded around the mid-7th century, and it rose to prominence as the largest West African empire by the 18th century, surpassing even Ife. This was due to the efforts of their kings, known as Alaafins. From its creation by Oranyan to the present day, it has grown to become the biggest Yoruba-speaking state, and it has political influence over a large portion of other Yorubaland kingdoms.

However, the early Oyo Kingdom, when compared to its other early counterparts such as Owu and Ila, was smaller in size and military might. It was essentially seen as the younger brother to the other Yoruba kingdoms. One of the reasons for this is that it was created after the major Yoruba kingdoms had become established.

But by the 17th century, the Oyo Empire had become stronger and wealthier, and it had a larger landmass. The capital of this blossoming empire was known as Oyo-Ile. However, it was known to their Hausa neighbors as Oyo Katunga. This new empire was comprised of several Yoruba-speaking peoples and non-Yoruba speaking peoples, like the

Nupe, Bariba, and Aja. The kingdom also expanded westward as far as the Aja country in Benin and part of the Ashanti Empire in the modern-day Republic of Togo.

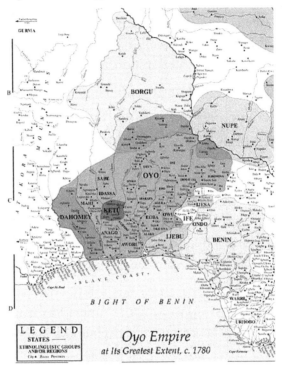

*The Oyo Empire at its greatest extent*

The Oyo Empire experienced a few setbacks during its journey to becoming a great power, but it became prominent through wealth gotten from trade with other neighboring kingdoms and Europeans. And with its powerful cavalry, they were able to dominate and conquer other African states.

*The Rise of the Oyo Empire*

In previous chapters, we talked about the first three kings of the Oyo Empire: Ajaka, Shango, and Aganju. You also might recall Oranyan, but it is important to note that he was not regarded as the first Alaafin despite founding the Oyo Empire. Instead, he was simply known as Oba Oranyan. There were many rulers of Oyo, such as

Oluaso, who is said to have had 1,460 children, but only the most influential will be discussed below.

## Ongibogi (r. c. 1500-c. 1537)

During his reign, the Oyo capital was besieged by the Nupe king. Around 1535, the Nupes occupied the capital, and many of the Oyos fled to Borgu, which was located in northwestern Nigeria.

## Eguguoju (ruled during the 16th century)

Eguguoju became the leader of the Oyo people while they were still in exile. The prior king, Onifran, had hoped to retake Oyo from the Nupe, and Eguguoju had the same dream. He and his followers camped in a forest on their way to Oyo. While Eguguoju was sitting at the foot of a tree, two birds, Igbo and Oyo, chased after each other from the top of the tree to the ground where Eguguoju was. He ordered that the birds be killed. This incident made him determined to fight to his last breath to regain Oyo.

When they reached Oyo, there was a ferocious battle against the Nupes. Eguguoju ended up moving the capital to Oyo Igboho ("New Oyo"). Some say that he named the capital after the birds who had inspired him to fight.

## Orompoto (r. c. 1554-c. 1562)

Orompoto was Eguguoju's sister, and she was the first woman to be the king of Oyo in the era of imperialism. She became the king because there was no male successor to take control of Oyo. According to some traditions, she transformed into a man before assuming the throne. She was a skilled warrior on horseback, and she drove the Nupes away from the capital in 1555. She also apparently displayed her bravery in the Battle of Ilayi.

In the battle, three of her war chiefs died. The last one fell on the ground, a grin still on his face. He looked as if he was still alive, so the Oyos' enemies thought that the chiefs were impossible to beat, and they fled the battlefield.

## Ajiboyede (ruled sometime during the 16<sup>th</sup> century)

Ajiboyede was the next Alaafin of Oyo. Early on in his reign, the Nupes again attacked the empire. Victory was on the side of the Nupe warriors until Ajanlapa, a court official, took a daring tactic. Ajanlapa told Ajiboyede to give him his crown and clothes to wear. Ajiboyede did this, and Ajanlapa ran toward the Nupes, making them think that he was the king. They shot arrows at him, and eventually, one fatally pierced him. The Nupes were wrong in thinking they had won, though; Ajanlapa's men quickly attacked the Nupe warriors and killed them.

Ajiboyede celebrated a festival called Bebe, which celebrated the defeat of the Nupes. The festival was held for many years after, and it gave the people the chance to take joy in the peace that now enveloped the empire. Due to this peace, commerce and agriculture began to boom, and the new capital of Igboho grew. As a result of this, two major markets were established, and the city became known for its acquisition of horses from Hausaland, located in sub-Saharan Africa.

## Abipa (ruled late 16<sup>th</sup> to early 17<sup>th</sup> century)

Abipa was the next Alaafin, and he was the son of Eguguoju. He wanted to fulfill his father's last request of taking the seat of government back to Oyo. However, apparently, not everyone agreed with this move. Abipa refused to listen to them, so they planned to do something to change his decision. When Abipa's scouting party reached Oyo-Ile, people came out at night with torches and roamed about the place. The scouts believed they were spirits that disapproved of moving the seat of government.

This devastated the king, and he didn't know what to do. However, he thought that something was up, so he sent some hunters to investigate the matter. They found out that they were not spirits but rather human beings. One of the hunters attempted to shoot one of the humans but changed his mind when the man begged to be spared.

There is a story that says the men who masqueraded as ghosts were taken before the king. The king's nobles acted as if they knew nothing about this, even though some of them definitely did. The king decided to hold this close to his chest until the court gathered for the Jakuta sacrifices, which were made to Shango. After they were done with the proceedings, they advanced to the banquet hall to dine. However, the usual servants didn't present the food and drinks. Instead, the men who had played ghosts were the ones who came out to serve them.

The noblemen were surprised, and everyone ate quietly. They parted without a farewell to the king. Those involved in the plot showed no remorse for what they did. Instead, they poisoned the king's adviser.

The seat of government was finally moved to Oyo-Ile. Abipa buried charms in different places so that the capital of Oyo would never be destroyed by war. A medicine man asked for a newborn baby to be used as the ingredient for the charm. At that time, Abipa's wife had just given birth, so he ordered that the baby be killed. Then he handed the dead baby to the medicine man to do with as he wished. This act won the hearts of many because they understood how difficult it was for Abipa to sacrifice his son for them.

After this incident, Oyo-Ile was never destroyed by war.

### Obalokun (ruled during the 17<sup>th</sup> century)

Obalokun's reign was a short one, but some interesting things happened during it. For instance, salt was first introduced into Yorubaland during his rule. Also, Obalokun was in direct communication with the king of France, and supposedly, both of them were friends. He sent eight hundred messengers to take presents to France, but he never heard of them again.

*Other Events during the Oyo Empire's Rise*

With its rearing expansion, the empire attempted to attack the Benin Empire between 1578 and 1608 (most likely during Abipa's reign or at least partly during his reign). Although their efforts failed at first, they eventually conquered the Benin Empire and made them pay tribute to Oyo. The Oyo Empire developed an efficient system of collecting tributes and sending them back to the capital. This system was executed through representatives, known as Ajele, who were sent to govern the conquered communities. The Ajele were controlled and kept in check by the royal messengers known as the Ilari. All of this was backed up by an efficient military that was personally controlled by the Alaafin.

The efficient organization of the Oyo Empire in managing its conquered regions and communities boosted its rise. These regions were seen as being part of a larger entity. Since the empire had roots connecting them to Ile-Ife, its influence also spread to southern Yorubaland.

The areas under the control of the Oyo Empire can be divided into four main parts: metropolitan Oyo, where the capital was situated; Yorubaland; Ajaland, which was near the Kingdom of Benin; and the Egbado Corridor, located southwest of Yorubaland. All of these states practiced the same system of government, which was dictated by the capital of Oyo, making them a well-oiled machine for easy control by the Alaafin and his representatives.

Aside from its military advantage, the Oyo Empire's geographical location made it an important trading route, connecting many regional locations. They were also able to control and direct the volume of trade with the Hausa and people from Gao and Timbuktu. Significant amounts of Oyo textiles and iron products were sent to these regions in exchange for horses. These horses were used mainly for military purposes. The Oyos also controlled the slave trade to other West African states and kingdoms. This control over trading made the Oyo Empire extremely wealthy, and it significantly accelerated the development of the empire, both economically and militarily.

# Factors That Contributed to the Rise of the Oyo Empire

A lot of factors helped shape Oyo into a military and economic powerhouse. One factor that helped this tiny kingdom initially was the adversity and destruction it faced from its neighbors. This might sound like the opposite of helping, but it played a major role in how Oyo developed.

The capital's location made it a prime target for the Nupes and the Bariba people of Borgu from the northeast and northwest, respectively. These kingdoms were already well established in the region. They did not specifically target only Oyo-Ile, as they also attacked other Yoruba kingdoms as well.

This leads into yet another factor that aided in the development of Oyo, with both factors going hand in hand with each other. This second factor was the location of their capital: Oyo-Ile. The kingdom was located along one of the oldest trade routes, and it connected the forests and grasslands of central West Africa to the middle Niger. This made it a desirable spot for any ambitious kingdom. The new capital was attacked and threatened so much that it paid a lot of tribute to the Nupe and Bariba people in the north and the Owu Kingdom in the south. Although the Oyos lost Oyo-Ile, they eventually got it back, and they chased away their enemies.

The Oyo people knew they had to change their ways in order to survive and put a stop to all these attacks. So, the Oyos learned extensively from their neighbors by examining their efficient centralized system of government and strong military. The Oyos now knew they had to establish a military that would subdue and deter any attacks on them. Unlike other Yoruba kingdoms, Oyo-Ile overcame these problems and eventually became a recognized empire with military and economic strength.

Also, the location of Oyo-Ile provided a defensive cover that prevented its enemies from attacking it. It was located in a spot where natural barriers made it almost impregnable to outside forces. The range of rocky hills surrounding the city made the maneuverability of enemy forces difficult, making the city less accessible for a direct attack. Asides from this natural barrier, the people built great walls around the city, and for nearly two centuries, no enemy came directly to the capital.

Agriculture was another factor that greatly assisted in the rise of the Oyo Empire. The city was situated in a region favorable for growing crops. The savannah grassland and its low rolling hills provided fertile soil for crops. Also, the region possessed streams that served as a good water source, with the Osun River flowing from the south and the Niger River coming from the north.

Farming on a larger scale allowed for a rapid increase in the population of the capital, which leads us to the next factor: a rise in the population. By the late 15th century, the Oyo cities were easily the most populated cities in Yorubaland; this allowed for the easy recruitment of men, and it ultimately helped build their military into an all-conquering army.

In addition to farming, another advantage provided by the savannah grassland was the use of horses, which they received from trading with the Hausas in the north. Horses allowed for easier communication and transportation over long distances. This also became a military advantage, and it helped the growing kingdom subdue its neighbors.

Horses aided in establishing administrative and commercial actions that could have been a nightmare for such a large empire. It also enabled them to conquer and control lands that were far from the capital. Oyo officials were often aware of the happenings in distant areas.

The control of commerce in the region also played into the hands of the Oyo people since their capital was established along important and well-known trade routes. The Oyos dominated the trading world compared to other kingdoms during its peak in the 18th century. They traded embroidery with the Hausas in the north in exchange for horses. Furthermore, they traded iron tools with Ajaland in the south. They were also heavily involved in the slave trade and were one of the first kingdoms to trade slaves with the Europeans. The large volume of trade controlled by the empire brought enormous wealth to the empire and its people.

Another contributing factor to the rise of the Oyo Empire was the general acceptance and support it had from other Yoruba kingdoms. Kingdoms like Owu and Ila suffered from raids and attacks from the Nupes and Bariba people as well, and they saw the breakthrough of Oyo as more of a success than as another source of competition. The Alaafin was part of the Yoruba kingship family who came from Ile-Ife, so his success and influence were seen as that of an influential member and as something not to be feared but embraced.

At the height of the Oyo Empire's power, the Alaafin even acted as an intermediary in disputes between other Yoruba kingdoms. These kingdoms offered support, hospitality, and supplies to Oyo soldiers conducting military campaigns in far-away regions. One good example is Ila, where their king provided aid to Oyo troops while fighting against the Nupe people. Oyo reciprocated by allowing easy trade and travel into its territories. This close relationship with other Yoruba kingdoms bolstered the Alaafin's influence. All of these factors aided in the military, economic, and political rise of the Oyo Empire.

## Political Life in the Oyo Empire

During the glory days of the Oyo Empire, the political situation ensured that prosperity was certain. Unlike most of the other Yoruba kingdoms, the Oyo people developed a sophisticated political structure that ensured checks and balances for a smooth transition of power and eliminated abuse by the Alaafin. This helped them to govern their conquered domains effectively.

The typical Yoruba system of government was employed in the Oyo Empire, with the head being the Alaafin. The Alaafin was chosen from a pool of princes who were descended from Oranyan. However, the first son of the king was not included in this pool. If you can call recall, the first son was known as the Aremo, and he had to die by committing suicide when his father died. This was because succession by primogeniture was largely rejected by the Yoruba kingdoms. This practice was later abandoned.

The kingmakers, known as the Oyo Mesi, were established to enthrone a king and also dethrone him by giving him an empty calabash or a dish of parrot eggs, thereby forcing him to commit suicide. (It should be noted that the Oyo Mesi is still around today, but it takes more of a ceremonial role.) The Oyo Mesi were seven councilors, consisting of the Agbaakin, the Samu, the Alapini, the Laguna, the Akiniku, and the Ashipa. They were all led by the Bashorun. They acted like politicians with electoral and legislative powers, which prevented the Alaafin from being an absolute ruler with infinite power. Each councilor had a specific duty to perform at court each day.

While the chiefs that made up the Oyo Mesi might not have been from the royal bloodline, they assisted the Alaafin in governing the kingdom. They made decisions and laws for the good of the kingdom. In civic ceremonies, the Alaafin had the power of life and death over his subjects, but in reality, the ruler was subject to the Oyo Mesi.

In line with the empire's military policy, the Oyo Mesi were also military chiefs. The officer presiding over the Oyo Mesi was the Bashorun, who held the highest office among the council. His responsibility was akin to that of a prime minister, and he controlled the army. The Laguna acted more in an ambassadorial role for the empire. The Alapini was in charge of the religious affairs of the state, especially the Egungun festival and the Ifa cult. These festivals and practices were the accepted state religion.

In choosing a king, the Bashorun had to consult the Ifa oracle before selecting a new Alaafin, who generally came from one of the three royal houses. Although the position of the king was not necessarily hereditary, the successors still had to be a descendant of Oranyan.

As powerful as the Oyo Mesi may appear, their power was also checked. The Ogboni might not have had any political or administrative authority, but it was backed by religion. Since the group primarily consisted of old sages noted for their knowledge in religious and political affairs, it was highly regarded by the people, so it was able to influence the Oyo Mesi's decisions and have direct access to the Alaafin on matters of the state.

Though the military was controlled by the Alaafin, it was still involved in checking the control of powerful individuals. Soldiers could be used to compel and dissuade a tyrannical Alaafin or even the Oyo Mesi into changing their opinions about matters of state.

Palace affairs were controlled by many high- and low-ranked officials that numbered up to a hundred. These officials attended to the king's needs and that of his family as well. They also tended to the palace and ensured daily rituals were done properly. Eunuchs, whose presence was uncommon in other Yoruba cultures, attended to the king's wives and children.

Outside the empire's capital of Oyo-Ile, the other conquered regions were governed by individuals appointed by the Alaafin. They served as his representative in the region and carried out his instructions. These conquered regions were supposed to serve the capital by providing goods, services, humans, and material resources. At the peak of its power, the Oyo Empire was comprised of many tributary states.

# The Notorious Alaafins of the Oyo Empire

Although it seems like most of the rulers of Oyo looked out for the interests of the people, that was certainly not the case. Some rulers were tyrants who pushed the envelope on what they could do to demonstrate their power. We have selected three rulers of Oyo and included the various legends surrounding their reign. It might seem that these men brought about the decline of the empire, but that was not the case. You will notice that all of them ended up either dying in battles to retain their power or committing ritual suicide, as the people held their kings to a higher standard.

### Karan

The dates of Karan's reign are not known, but he succeeded Odarawu, who ruled during the late 17th century. He was a tyrant and the worst of them all. He was so cruel to his subjects that his name was attached to a saying: "as cruel as Karan."

A conspiracy began when he sent an expedition to Aga Oibo. At some point, the people on the expedition had rebellious thoughts and were ready for action. It was made known to them by divination that Karan couldn't be conquered unless they offered his fan-bearer as a sacrifice to the gods. They sent a message to him requesting his fan-bearer, and he agreed.

After they sacrificed the fan-bearer to the gods, they sent back meat. Karan ate it, and they declared that Karan's words no longer had value since he had just eaten his servant. Hence, his army would no longer be charged with disobedience if they decided to go against him.

Karan's death was demanded, but he didn't want to go down without a fight. Even though the whole army was against him, he shot arrows at them until his hands were swollen. He climbed to the top of the roof to continue shooting, but the people burned the palace. He died in the fire.

### Jayin

Jayin was next in line, and he was the son of Alaafin Karan. He wasn't much different from his tyrannical father. Olusi, his son, had a tender and caring personality. Everyone depended on Olusi to give the country a better future, but he fell under the charms of one of his father's wives. His father was already jealous of Olusi's popularity, and once this happened, Jayin decided he had to take drastic actions.

One version explained that while his father reprimanded him, Jayin had a club in his hand, and the top of the club was spiked with poison. He drove the club into Olusi's head, and Olusi didn't survive.

Another version says Olusi was given poisoned bean cakes by his father, which killed him. Either way, Olusi died because his father poisoned him.

Olusi was gravely mourned, and the chiefs wanted to find out who was behind his death because they couldn't believe Jayin's story that his son's death was due to a kick from his horse. The truth was eventually spilled by one of the wives, and this made the chiefs hate the king.

Apparently, chanters approached the palace. Jayin heard them, and he thought it was best to kill himself before the chanters began incorporating his cruel act into their songs.

### Ayibi (ruled during the 17<sup>th</sup> century)

Ayibi was crowned when he was old enough. However, he disappointed his people because he had no respect for them and took pleasure in shedding blood. Whenever a case was brought to him, he always ordered the execution of both the complainant and the defendant. He never respected anyone, even those older than him in age and rank.

One day, he was with his wife in the bath when she made a statement. "And this is all of the man dreaded by all." He didn't like what she had said, but he covered his displeasure with a smile. After he left the bathroom, he privately told an executioner to fetch the head of his wife's mother and father and place them in calabashes.

The executioner did this and brought the calabashes to him. Ayibi sent for his wife and told her to open them. She did so, and he asked her if she knew them. With tears in her eyes, she said she knew them. Then he said, "That is the reason I am so much dreaded by all, although to you I am commonplace and ordinary." She expected him to kill her, but he disappointed her. Instead, he loved the misery he saw in her eyes.

His cruelty made the city reject him, and because of this, he committed suicide.

It might not make much sense to people today that people as dreaded as Ayibi, Jayin, and Shango committed suicide. But the reason almost all rejected kings committed suicide was that anyone who was proclaimed as king was sacred and venerated by the gods. The moment his followers spoke the words "We reject you," he must die by his own hands. This was because a king could not return to being a private individual or continue ruling after making his followers suffer.

The people would prefer not to kill the Alaafin because he was sacred; instead, he had to kill himself. If the king killed himself, he would have an honorable burial. But if he didn't, and the people eventually killed him, his corpse would be treated like garbage, and his house would be pulled down. Hence, most of them decide to commit suicide for the sake of their relatives.

# The Fall of the Oyo Empire

The Oyo Empire served as a representative measure for the other Yoruba kingdoms since it was the largest and most dominant for centuries. It could also be said that its fall from grace affected the other Yoruba kingdoms too. The decline of this glorious empire began in early 1754 when the power-hungry Bashorun, Gaha, started a coup that led to the empire's demise. He conspired with the other Oyo Mesi and the Ogboni to remove four successive Alaafins from the throne by forcing them to commit suicide. They presented all of them with a calabash containing parrot eggs.

Bashorun Gaha's hold on the throne was only broken during the reign of Alaafin Abiodun. In 1774, Abiodun executed Gaha due to his constant plotting and scheming. However, the cracks brought about during the tumultuous reign of Gaha never really closed; rather, they widened, which ultimately led to the collapse of the Oyo Empire.

After overcoming Bashorun Gaha, Alaafin Abiodun conducted raids against Borgu (home of the Bariba). They all failed, which led to a decline in the Alaafin's popularity. After Abiodun's death, his son or cousin, Awole, assumed the throne. These events begin a chain of cataclysmic actions, starting with the breakaway of Ilorin led by Kakanfo Afonja.

What happened next was described in the prior chapter, but eventually, Awole committed suicide. After Awole's death, Oyo declined into civil war, with numerous factions fighting for the throne. With a weakened Oyo Mesi, this civil war escalated, and for almost twenty years, the factions could not agree on a new Alaafin. This power tussle created a huge vacuum in a capital already filled with powerful military commanders. It also led to the separation of Ilorin from Oyo in 1817. Ilorin did not remain independent for long, though. Alimi killed Afonja, and in 1823, Ilorin became part of the Sokoto Caliphate, which had been founded in 1804 during the Fulani Wars.

By 1825, the Oyo Empire was a shadow of its former self. Alaafin Majotu (r. 1802–1830) sought the help of the British and the Oba of Benin in putting down the rebellions caused by Ilorin. Part of the problem was that the Oyos no longer had full access to their soldiers, as many of them, as well as horses, had been stationed in Ilorin, which was now under the control of the Muslims. The Alaafin was also made to convert to Islam.

Ilorin destroyed many Oyo villages in its attempt to take over the empire. Eventually, the Muslims reached the capital of Oyo-Ile and destroyed it in 1835. The destruction of Oyo-Ile by the Fulanis led to the capital being moved south to Ago d'Oyo. This action led to a shift in power to Ibadan, which was already a settlement for war generals. This action would be the straw that broke the camel's back. The Oyo Empire never regained its authority and importance in Yorubaland. In 1888, Oyo became one of Great Britain's protectorates.

It was easy for Britain to gain access to Yorubaland due to the role it played during the slave trade. Europeans, such as Hugh Clapperton, who were interested in legitimate trade after the abolishment of the slave trade in 1807, toured Yorubaland and Hausaland. The exploration of the regions laid the path for British colonization.

In 1914, while Oyo was under colonial rule, the Province of Oyo was created, and it constituted Oyo, Ilesha, Ife, and Ila. Oyo Province was surrounded by Ilorin to the north; Abeokuta, Ijebu-Ode, and Ondo to the south; Dahomey to the west; and Kontagora to the east. The monarchs of the four Oyo Province kingdoms continued ruling.

Colonization facilitated the improvement of trade, sanitization, and the development of better structures. Schools, pharmacies, town halls, hospitals, and post offices were built. With advanced knowledge of architecture and modifications to suit the weather from the British, new residential structures were put in place.

The first native school was introduced in 1928. The British colonizers focused on advancing the "primitive but progressive" Yorubas in terms of science, language, and religion. British teachers were present to teach the English language. Christian missionaries were also present in the schools to convert the young children to the new religion, and they were taught to pass the message to their parents. Christianity was fiercely resisted by the elders in the communities, as the religion went against their traditional practices and ways of living. But as Western ideas of rationalism and individualism became more pronounced among the educated, they began to replace the traditional teachings, allowing Christianity to take hold.

# Chapter 8 – Folklore Stories

Yoruba folk tales were passed down through the generations. It was an effective way of not forgetting the customs, as well as imbibing moral lessons in order to better handle whatever life may throw at them.

Here are some of the stories told in ancient and modern-day Yorubaland.

### Akiti the Hunter

Akiti was a hunter known to have conquered man and animal alike. No animal crossed his path and went scot-free, be it snakes, lions, wolves, or leopards. Because of this, he called himself the "King of the Forest."

His triumph over animals made him prideful, and everyone feared him. He had forgotten that there was one animal that he had not yet encountered—the elephant.

The elephant was angry that Akiti was calling himself king because the elephant was already known to be the King of the Forest. So, the elephant challenged Akiti to a battle. Akiti threw a sharp spear at the elephant, but the elephant's hide protected it. Then Akiti used his knife, bow, and poisoned arrows, but his efforts were worthless.

Seeing that the elephant had a charm that protected it from weapons, Akiti used his charm to turn into a lion and lunged toward the elephant. The elephant simply threw him off.

Next, he changed into a snake, but he was unsuccessful in crushing the elephant to death. Finally, he transformed into a fly and flew into the elephant's ear, deep into the elephant's heart. Then he drove his hunting knife through its heart. The elephant didn't survive this one.

At last, no one questioned Akiti's name. He was truly the King of the Forest.

### The Iroko Tree

There was a time when the Yorubas avoided the big tree in the forest. The tree referred to as "Iroko" was avoided because an old man inhabited it. At night, the old man walked around, shining his torch and instilling fear in travelers. Anyone that saw the old Iroko-man ran away from him as if they were mad and died soon after.

The thickness of the Iroko made the tree appealing to woodcutters, but they encountered misfortune when cutting it down, as their attempts caused them and their families to experience bad omens every day.

Every piece of furniture produced with Iroko-wood always groans and creaks at night. These noises are due to the old man trying to escape so that he can wander about again.

### Why Women Have Long Hair

Once upon a time, two women quarreled, and one of them decided to make the other suffer. She dug a hole in the middle of the road leading from the other woman's house to the village well. The next morning, the other woman followed her friends to fetch water. While they were traveling, she fell into the pit. She screamed for help, and her friends came to rescue her. They managed to grip her by the hair and draw her up. But the more they pulled at her hair, the more her hair stretched.

They succeeded in pulling her out, but she was ashamed of how her hair was as long as her arm, so she ran away to hide. Later on, she noticed that her long hair was beautiful, and she swelled with pride. She began to shun the women with short hair. This made the short-haired women jealous and ashamed of themselves.

So, each of them jumped into the pit while their friends pulled them out by their hair. This stretched their hair as well. After this, every woman was born with long hair.

### The Leopard Man

A beautiful stranger strolled about a village and never uttered a word. The maidens in the village were in love with him and wished to be his bride. Soon after, he disappeared into the forest.

One month later, he came in sight again, and one of the maidens who was in love with him followed him into the forest. He noticed her following him, and he turned around and begged her to go back. She refused and said, "I will never leave you, and wherever you go, I will follow."

"Beautiful maiden, you will regret it," he said as he trotted on. Both of them went deep into the forest and stopped at a tree with a leopard skin laid at its foot. He explained to her that he was allowed to go about the village once a month as a man but that he was actually a leopard. He told her that once he changed into his natural form, he would tear her into pieces.

Once he put the skin on, he immediately changed into a leopard and chased after her. The maiden was very fast, probably due to adrenaline, so it was difficult for him to catch her. As he chased her, he sang that he would tear her into pieces while she sang that he would never catch her.

A while later, she came across a river, and it seemed as if he would catch her after all. However, a tree by the corner of the river pitied her and bent over so she could cross the river. Finally, she reached the end of the forest and entered the village. The leopard was sad that he couldn't catch his prey and disappeared into the forest, never to be seen again.

## The Three Deaths of Tortoise

Many animals hated Tortoise, and they planned to kill him. While he was asleep one night, they set his hut on fire. As the flames roared, they were convinced that he could not escape and said to themselves, "He cannot escape. He will die."

Tortoise had coiled himself into his shell and wasn't scarred by the fire. The next morning, they were surprised to see him walking the streets of the village. Then they gathered for another plan, and this time, they flung Tortoise into a pool of water. They said to themselves, "The pool is deep. He will drown."

Tortoise pulled himself into his shell and didn't drown. At noon, the sun shone strongly and dried the pool. His enemies were again surprised to see him again walking the streets of the village as though nothing had happened.

They had already come up with another plan by the next day. This time, they were certain that he would not escape. They dug a deep pit in the ground and buried Tortoise. They put a bamboo stake in the spot to mark the place.

A man passing by saw the bamboo stake and thought someone had buried treasure there. So, he called his friends to help him dig. They dug and dug and found Tortoise asleep in his shell. Tortoise walked about the village with excitement, once more surprising his enemies.

They finally gave up, saying to themselves, "He has a charm, and we shall never be able to kill him."

## How The Leopard Got His Spots (Version 1)

The leopard didn't always have spots; once upon a time, his skin color was like that of a lion. But one day, Akiti the Hunter chased after him, and he was afraid that Akiti would kill him. So, he ate the root of a magic plant so that he would remain unaffected by Akiti's weapons.

Not long after, Akiti saw him among the trees and shot poisoned arrows at him, but the leopard escaped. These poisoned arrows created black spots on his body, allowing him to blend amongst the trees with the help of the sun and the shadows.

This makes it difficult for hunters to catch him even today.

### How The Leopard Got His Spots (Version 2)

Before, the leopard had very dark skin. He was strolling one day in a compound when he noticed a woman bathing in a hut. The leopard circled the hut, waiting for his prey to step out. But he was very hungry and couldn't wait anymore. He went into the hut, shocking the woman to her bones. She screamed in fear and threw her loofah filled with soap at him.

He fled, covered with soap from head to foot, which he still has on to this very day.

### Isokun and the Baby

Dekun, a king, had a wife called Isokun. She bore him no children, which created sadness and tension in the palace. One day, Isokun went missing. Everyone searched for her, but no one could find her. They didn't know that she had gone to plead with the gods of the land for a child. She went far and wide, but none of the gods had pity on her.

She headed back to her village, devastated by the gods' refusal. On her way, she saw an old woman asleep by the road with her two-day-old baby. Isokun stole the baby and hurried to the palace. She explained to the king that she went to the gods to give her a child and that her prayers were answered. The palace rejoiced. Sacrifices were made, and a great feast ensued.

The real mother finally woke up and saw that her baby was gone. Her efforts to find her baby were futile, but she was not ready to give up. She continued her search until she got to the palace. It was easy for her to enter because of the feast that was taking place.

The baby had been crying because of hunger, and Isokun could not feed him. She was unsuccessful in trying to pacify him without being suspicious. The old woman, drawn by the baby's noise, snatched the baby from Isokun and breastfed him, which comforted him immediately.

A few moments later, everyone knew that Isokun had lied. The old woman left with her baby, and Isokun fled the palace because she feared the king's anger. She never returned.

### The Ants and the Treasure

There was a very poor man that cared for animals. Even though he had very little, he always left grains of corn and beans for his parrot. To pacify the ants from attacking his few possessions, he always spread tidbits of these grains on the floor, hoping it would be enough for them.

The ants were grateful for his actions.

In the same village, there was a rich man who refused to spend his money. He had stolen someone's gold and kept it in the corner of his hut. He watched over it day and night. Every living thing that crossed his path he killed and crushed, even the birds and the ants. He hated everything except his gold.

This angered the ants because he had killed a substantial number of their kind, so they decided to punish him. After discussing it, they came up with an idea. They wanted to take the gold to the poor man's house. So, they dug a tunnel, with one end at the poor man's house and the other at the rich man's house.

The very night that they completed the tunnel, a large swarm of ants carried a part of the gold through the tunnel to the poor man's house. The following day, the poor man was very excited that the gods had sent the gold. He kept the gold in a corner and covered it with a cloth.

Meanwhile, the rich man had discovered that a huge part of the gold was gone. He was confused as to how it had happened because he kept watch all night. The next night, the ants carried another part of the gold down the tunnel. Again, the poor man was happy, while the rich man was furious.

The third night, the ants successfully moved all of the gold from the rich man's home to the poor man's house. The rich man was devastated and called his neighbors. He explained how his gold had disappeared in three days. He emphasized that no one had entered his hut and that he was certain that it was stolen through witchcraft.

They helped him search his house and discovered the tunnel. Obviously, someone had stolen it through the tunnel, so they went through the tunnel to discover its other end. They found the poor man's house and discovered the gold.

The poor man protested that he couldn't have stolen it through a small tunnel. The rich man's neighbors accused him of using witchcraft to make himself small and stealing the gold at night. They punished him by shutting him in his hut. The next day, they decided to burn him alive.

When the ants saw what had happened, they were baffled and thought of how to help their friend from being executed. There was no other option than for them to eat the hut. This they did in a few hours, and the poor man was dazed to find himself in an open space. But he didn't think twice. He escaped into the forest, never to return again.

The next morning, the villagers came and saw that the ants had been responsible for releasing the man. They thought the gods had taken the punishment into their own hands by sending the ants to eat both the hut and the poor man.

Until today, only the ants know that's not the truth.

### The Head

In a certain village, the villagers coexisted without bodies. They had only heads. They moved about by jumping, so they never went far.

One of the heads wished to see the world, so he left the village one morning in secret. He met a woman who was looking out the window and asked if she could lend him a torso. The woman agreed. She lent him the torso of her slave, and the head thanked her and went on his way.

Later, he met a man sleeping under the tree and asked if he could lend him his arms since the man wasn't using them. The man agreed and lent him his arms. The head thanked him and went on his way.

Later on, he stopped at a river where some fishermen were singing and fishing. He asked if one of them could lend him a pair of legs as they were sitting and not using their legs at that moment. One of the men agreed and lent the adventurous man his legs. He thanked the man and went on his way.

Now, his body was complete. He had a torso, arms, legs, and a head.

He headed to a village, where onlookers tossed coins to maidens as the maidens danced. He tossed all his coins to a maiden, and she admired his handsomeness. She asked him to marry her and take her to his village.

He married the lady, and they set out the next day. When they reached the riverbank, he pulled off the legs and gave them to the fisherman. Later, they reached the tree where that man was still sleeping, and the head gave his arms back to him. Finally, they reached the cottage where he met the woman and gave her the torso.

When the maiden saw that he was just a head, she was terrified and ran as fast as she could. Since the head had no arms, legs, or body, he couldn't catch her, so he lost her forever.

### Erin and Erinomi (The Land and the Water Elephants)

The tortoise was known to cause trouble amongst the animals. One day, while walking alongside the river, the tortoise met the elephant and told him, "The hippo brags that you are weak and cannot even muster the strength to haul a log of wood from the water."

"That is not true!" the elephant cried. To prove how strong he was, the elephant told the tortoise to bind a piece of twine to his trunk and fix the other end to a tree. The tortoise did as he was told, then went down to the river and pulled the same prank on the hippo. The tortoise started by saying that, "The elephant is boastful of his strength and proclaims you a weakling that cannot fell a tree."

Surprised, the hippo cried, "That is not true! I can bring down any tree." Then the tortoise told him that he had fastened twine to a tree and that he could bind the other end to the hippo. The hippo agreed to tie the twine to his tusk.

The animals pulled and pulled, one at each end, but neither gave way. After a while, the hippo decided to rest. And the elephant decided to go to the river to drink some water. There, they found that the tortoise had deceived them. Angrily, they searched all over for the tortoise, but he was already long gone.

# Conclusion

After Nigeria was liberated in 1960, the surviving ancient Yoruba kingdoms maintained their monarchs, but today, many of the rulers do not have the power their ancestors used to wield. However, they are all respected by their subjects and are given honorary reverence by the government of Nigeria.

The kingdoms are not as big as they used to be because they have been divided into administrative boundaries (states) by the ruling government of Nigeria. The first division of Nigeria was done in 1967 by the military head of state, General Yakubu Gowon.

As mentioned in the book, Yorubas are all over the world. This is partially due to the slave trade but primarily due to the large rate of emigration of Africans from third-world countries to developed countries. The Yorubas got into the slave trade later than most, which resulted in many Yorubas still having knowledge of their culture and language when slavery was abolished. This allowed them to establish diaspora communities more easily after they were freed. Within these diaspora communities, they have kept their culture and are known for their different traditional attires and parties, which are known as *owambes.*

There is at least one Yoruba person in almost every country, and coupled with their love for promoting their culture and their language, the Yorubas are very popular. They are also known to be disciplined, hardworking, and industrious.

This comprehensive book draws on rare historical books, documentaries, and revelations from people to cover the origin of the Yoruba people and their ancestral heroes, traditions, economy, and politics.

It is important to note that the stories, events, and figures in this book are just a glimpse of who the Yoruba people actually are. There are still many aspects of their history that are yet to be told. However, we hope this book achieved its aim of providing a captivating introductory guide through the history of the Yoruba people.

# Free Bonus from Captivating History (Available for a Limited time)

Hi History Lovers!

Now you have a chance to join our exclusive history list so you can get your first history ebook for free as well as discounts and a potential to get more history books for free! Simply visit the link below to join.

Captivatinghistory.com/ebook

Also, make sure to follow us on Facebook, Twitter and Youtube by searching for Captivating History.

Here's another book by Captivating History that you might like

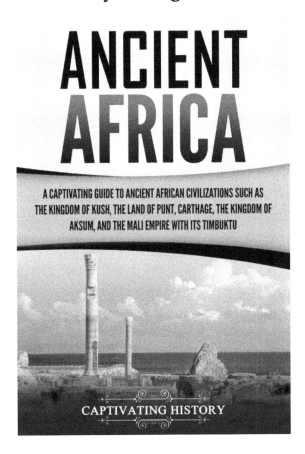

ANCIENT AFRICA

A CAPTIVATING GUIDE TO ANCIENT AFRICAN CIVILIZATIONS SUCH AS THE KINGDOM OF KUSH, THE LAND OF PUNT, CARTHAGE, THE KINGDOM OF AKSUM, AND THE MALI EMPIRE WITH ITS TIMBUKTU

CAPTIVATING HISTORY

# References

"Yoruba Religion." https://en.m.wikipedia.org/wiki/Yoruba_religion

"Yoruba Folk Tales." https://yorubafolktales.wordpress.com

"Oduduwa." https://en.m.wikipedia.org/wiki/Oduduwa

Sheriff, Oshin. "Sango, the Yoruba God of Thunder and Lightning." March 2018. https://medium.com/@OGBENISKILLA/sango-the-yoruba-god-of-thunder-and-lightning-99e8111c10d2

"Ogun." https://en.m.wikipedia.org/wiki/Ogun

"Oshun." https://en.m.wikipedia.org/wiki/Oshun

Akintoye, Stephen Adebanji. *A History of the Yoruba People.* 2010.

Ogundiran, Akinwumi. *The Yoruba: A New History.* November 2020.

Johnson, Samuel. *The History of the Yorubas from the Earliest Times to the Beginning of the British Protectorate.* First published 1921.

Printed in the USA
CPSIA information can be obtained
at www.ICGtesting.com
LVHW011553260923
759110LV00004B/126